# The Impact of Climate Policy on Environmental and Economic Performance

Sweden has a long history of ambitious environmental, energy, and climate policy. Due to the large amount of data available it is possible to perform statistically sound analysis and assess long-term changes in productivity, efficiency, and technological development. The data at hand together with Sweden's ambitious energy and climate policy provide a unique opportunity to shed light on pertinent policy issues.

*The Impact of Climate Policy on Environmental and Economic Performance* answers several key questions: What is the effect of the $CO_2$ tax on environmental performance and profitability of firms? Does including emissions in productivity measurement of the industrial firm matter? Did the introduction of the EU ETS spur technological development in the Swedish industrial firm? What air pollutant is most inhibiting production when regulated? Being aware and learning from the Swedish case can be very relevant for countries that are in the process of shaping their climate policy.

This book is of great importance to researchers and policy makers who are interested in environmental economics, industrial economics, and climate change.

**Rolf Färe** is a Professor of Economics and Applied Economics at Oregon State University. As a former student of Ronald W. Shephard, his main research interest is in production theory, especially in an activity analysis or DEA framework, and applications in numerous fields, including environmental economics, energy efficiency, and health. Since 2015 he has been an Adjunct Faculty at the Department of Agricultural and Resource Economics at the University of Maryland, USA.

**Shawna Grosskopf** is Professor Emerita and currently an adjunct professor at the Centre for Environmental and Resource Economics, Umeå, Sweden. Recent research has included work on using directional distance functions to model productivity in the presence of environmental byproducts and assessing performance in the health sector.

**Tommy Lundgren** is a Professor of Economics at the Centre for Environmental and Resource Economics, Umeå, Sweden. His research is mainly focused on applied policy analysis related to the environment. Currently, he is running a project assessing industrial energy demand and energy efficiency in Sweden.

**Per-Olov Marklund** is a Researcher at the National Institute of Economic Research (NIER), Stockholm, Sweden. His research focuses on applied policy analysis that relates to the environment. He is currently involved in research on green public procurement as an environmental policy instrument.

**Wenchao Zhou** is a Senior Researcher at Centre for Regional Sciences at Umeå University, Sweden.

# Routledge Explorations in Environmental Economics
Edited by Nick Hanley
*University of Stirling, UK*

*For a full list of titles in this series, please visit https://www.routledge.com/series/REEE*

# The Impact of Climate Policy on Environmental and Economic Performance

Evidence from Sweden

Rolf Färe, Shawna Grosskopf, Tommy Lundgren, Per-Olov Marklund, and Wenchao Zhou

LONDON AND NEW YORK

First published 2017
by Routledge
2 Park Square, Milton Park, Abingdon, Oxon OX14 4RN

and by Routledge
711 Third Avenue, New York, NY 10017

*Routledge is an imprint of the Taylor & Francis Group,
an informa business*

*British Library Cataloguing in Publication Data*
A catalogue record for this book is available from the British Library

*Library of Congress Cataloging-in-Publication Data*
A catalog record for this book has been requested

ISBN: 978-1-138-84747-7 (hbk)
ISBN: 978-1-315-72680-9 (ebk)

Typeset in Times New Roman
by Apex CoVantage, LLC

# Contents

# Figures

# Tables

# Preface

In late 2015, the twenty-first session of the UNFCCC Conference of the Parties (COP21) was held in Paris. The outcome of the conference, the Paris Agreement, is a legally binding treaty on climate action that includes commitments from most countries in the world and takes effect in 2020. The commitments are ambitious, and countries face major climate and energy policy challenges. In this context, this book sheds light on several important research questions.

We believe that the book can provide useful insights to any country in the process of shaping climate and energy policy. It brings forward not only empirical research on Swedish climate and energy policy and its outcome, which other countries could learn from, but also research methods that are generally applicable and can be employed in any country if adequate data is available.

The book summarizes a research project that took place during 2011–2013, and we would like to thank the Swedish Energy Agency for supporting the project. We would also like to thank Runar Brännlund at the Centre for Environmental and Resource Economics (CERE), Umeå University, Sweden, and Eva Samakovlis, Head of Division, Environmental Economics Research, at the Swedish National Institute of Economic Research (NIER). They co-authored two of the papers that the book is partly based on.

Umeå, Stockholm and Corvallis, March 31, 2016

Rolf Färe, Shawna Grosskopf, Tommy Lundgren,
Per-Olov Marklund, and Wenchao Zhou

# 1  Introduction

Sweden has a long history of environmental policy in general, and, in terms of addressing energy and climate policy and its effects on industrial firms, the amount of data is now sufficiently large to ask the relevant questions and perform statistically sound analysis. A relatively long period of firm-level data (1990–2008) available gives us the possibility to assess long-term changes in productivity, efficiency, and technological development, along with environmental performance. This panel data, together with Sweden's ambitious energy and climate policy, provide us a unique opportunity to shed light on pertinent issues of energy and climate policy through relevant analysis, both in theory and, most importantly, empirically.

The general aim of the book is to address the role of climate policy on Swedish industrial firms' environmental and economic performance. How has the Swedish carbon dioxide ($CO_2$) tax (introduced 1991) impacted environmental performance in terms of changing $CO_2$ emission intensity? What effect did the $CO_2$ tax have on efficiency and profitability of firms? Does it matter to include or not include air emissions in productivity measurement of the industrial firm? Did the introduction of the European Union Emissions Trading System (EU ETS) spur technological development in the Swedish industrial firms? What regulated air emission is most inhibiting production? These are examples of questions we want to shed light on in this book. To learn from the Swedish example, we believe, can therefore be very relevant for countries that are in the process of shaping their climate policy. The methods used in this book are generally applicable, and with adequate data they can be employed for analysis of similar issues in other countries as well.

Specifically, in the book we present:

- A comprehensive account and a summary of the research generated within the project titled "The impact of energy and climate policy on sustainability and competitiveness in Swedish industry" (supported by the Swedish Energy Agency 2011–2013).

- Research that is unique in terms of examining the role of policy by integrating theory and empirics using detailed and exclusive firm-level data from Swedish industry.
- Research that sheds light on the whole chain, from the effects of regulation and policy on environmental performance to the ultimate impact on economic performance.
- Research that deals with the long-debated question concerning whether regulation is associated with a no-cost (i.e., the Porter hypothesis, Porter and van der Linde, 1995) or a cost-benefit (e.g., Palmer et al., 1995) paradigm.

## 1.1   Policy background

Energy is an important factor in modern society, both in terms of input in production and consumption of various products. However, energy is also a critical component of the origins of environmental problems like climate change. It is also evident that different countries deal politically differently with these problems. In many countries, it is justified to re-evaluate policies to reduce $CO_2$ emissions at the lowest possible cost (OECD, 2013).

In this section, we first give a brief background to the Swedish energy and climate policy, followed by a brief and general discussion from an international perspective. Then, a short discussion on the EU ETS is provided. Finally, we give a presentation of the data that is analyzed.

### 1.1.1   Climate and energy policy in Sweden[1]

As early as in the 1920s, Sweden began to tax energy consumption for fiscal reasons. With the advent of the oil crisis in the 70s, there was a need to expand the energy taxation for energy policy purposes. In addition to reducing dependence on oil, the ambition was to increase consumption of electricity, mainly through the expansion of nuclear power. Later on, during the 80s, energy taxation began to be increasingly motivated by environmental reasons (Brännlund, 2009).

In the early 90s, a comprehensive tax reform was carried out in Sweden, which included reforming energy and environmental taxation. In 1991, a tax was set to SEK 30 per kilo emission sulfur dioxide ($SO_2$) from coal and peat, and to SEK 27 per cubic meter for each tenth of a percentage by mass of sulfur content in oil.[2,3] In 1992 was introduced a fiscally neutral fee on nitrogen oxides ($NO_x$) emission from large energy-producing combustion plants. The fee was set to SEK 40 per kilo emission (Swedish Environmental Protection Agency, 2003) and increased to SEK 50 in 2008 (Swedish Energy Agency, 2008).

In 1991, Sweden introduced a tax on $CO_2$, setting the tax rate to SEK 0.25 per kilo emission (Swedish Energy Agency, 2006).[4] In 1993, an energy tax reform that led to substantial increases in energy and $CO_2$ tax rates was carried out. However, in order to reduce the burden from taxation, the manufacturing industry was exempted from paying energy tax and needed to pay only 25 percent of the statutory $CO_2$ tax rate. One reason for this was to avoid major consequences for the industry's competitiveness on international markets (Brännlund, 2009). The 1993 year tax increases mainly affected households. However, in 1997, the $CO_2$ tax that industry needed to pay was increased to 50 percent of the statutory $CO_2$ tax rate (Statistics Sweden, 2000). Furthermore, during the 2000s the statutory tax rate was increased substantially, stepwise from SEK 0.37 in 2000 to SEK 0.91 in 2004 to SEK 1.01 in 2008. The tax rate was further increased in 2009 to SEK 1.05, in 2014 to SEK 1.08, and in 2015 to SEK 1.12. For those industries included in the EU ETS, however, the $CO_2$ tax was gradually phased out starting in 2008 and completely removed at the end of 2010.

The energy tax payment exemption for the manufacturing industry was removed in 2004, in connection with an energy tax being levied on electricity use in production. The tax rate was set to the minimum requirement according to the EU Energy Tax Directive, i.e., SEK 0.005 per kWh.[5]

In 2005, the Swedish Energy Efficiency Improvement Program (PFE) was introduced to encourage energy-intensive firms within manufacturing to invest in energy saving measures and increase energy efficiency in the production processes (Swedish Energy Agency, 2010). By voluntarily joining the program, firms have the opportunity to be exempted from the energy tax. The first period of the program, concluded at the end of 2009, resulted in annual savings of 1.45 TWh.[6] The second period is currently underway and expected to be fully completed in 2017.[7] However, due to the design of the program, significant energy efficiency investments are not realized. (Mansikkasalo and Söderholm, 2013). In this respect, energy efficiency programs could possibly be more successful if explicitly targeted at promoting technological development (Blomberg et al., 2012).

### 1.1.2  An international perspective

Based on statutory tax rates on 1 April 2012, OECD (2013) shows that effective tax rates differ considerably between OECD countries. For instance, the lowest and highest tax rates per ton of $CO_2$, EUR 2.80 and EUR 107.28, are found in Mexico and Switzerland, respectively. The top five countries with the highest $CO_2$ tax rates after Switzerland are

Luxembourg, the Netherlands, and the Nordic countries of Norway, Denmark, and Sweden.

In general, the highest effective tax rates tend to be in EU Member States. Among these states, energy policy is essentially governed by the 2003 EU Energy Tax Directive. Countries with explicit $CO_2$ tax rates, such as Switzerland, Norway, Denmark, Sweden, Ireland, and Iceland, also tend to have high effective carbon tax rates. In these countries, $CO_2$ taxation generally is implemented along with, e.g., taxation of energy content in fuels (OECD, 2013).

Lower effective $CO_2$ tax rates are typically found in Central European and Asian OECD countries, e.g., Czech Republic, Estonia, Hungary, Japan, Korea, Poland, Slovak Republic, and Turkey. The lowest $CO_2$ tax rates were found in the American countries—United States, Canada, Chile, and Mexico (mentioned earlier)—and Australia[8] and New Zealand. Typical for the countries with the lowest tax rates is that they only tax fuels used in transport (OECD, 2013).

Sweden was one of the first countries to implement a direct tax on $CO^2$ emissions and is also one of the countries with high tax rate. However, Sweden is also part of the EU ETS.

### 1.1.3   EU Emissions Trading System

The European Union Emissions Trading System (EU ETS) was started 1 January 2005, allowing firms to trade EU Allowances Units (EUAs).[9] A cap on allowances was set for each individual EU Member State, one allowance corresponding to one ton of $CO_2$. The first period of trade ran until 2007, and the second until 2012.[10]

Launching the first period of trade, all EUAs were distributed free of charge to power plants and energy-intensive industries. The total volume of allowances was reduced when launching the second period of trade; most of the allowance was still distributed free of charge.[11],[12]

The data used in the empirical analyses presented in this book addresses the Swedish manufacturing sector and covers the first period of EU ETS and the first year of the second period. Significant for the first period was that a surplus of allowances compared to actual $CO_2$ emission caused by this sector was allocated (Swedish National Audit Office, 2012). Surplus allocation occurred generally within the EU, which, together with the fact that the allocated allowances expired at the end of 2007, had consequences for the EUA carbon price. As Figure 1.1 shows, the price peaked in early 2006, after which it fell considerably. For much of 2007, the price was closed to zero.

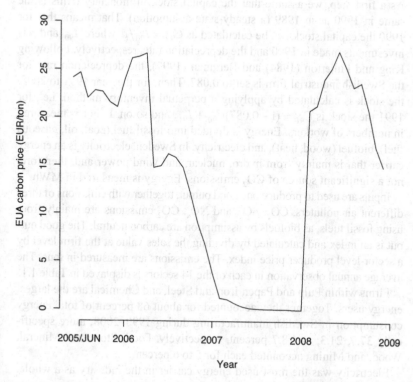

*Figure 1.1* Tendency of EUA carbon price based on monthly observed data, current prices

Source: www.bluenext.eu[13]

## 1.2 Data

In this book, we present results from our empirical work that addresses the effects of energy and climate policy on firm's environmental and economic performance in the Swedish manufacturing industry. The data used in the empirical analyses covers 14 sectors during the period from 1990 to 2008 and is especially compiled by Statistics Sweden (www.scb.se). The data is at the firm level and includes information on accounting variables (profit, salaries, value added, number of employees, etc.), energy use, emissions to air, environmental investment and expenditure, and energy and climate taxes.

The specific variables used in the analyses are as follows. Inputs used in manufacturing are capital, labor, and energy. The data does not include adequate information about the capital stock, and it is therefore calculated.

As a first step, we assume that the capital stock in monetary terms is the same in 1990 as in 1989 (a steady-state assumption). That means that for 1990 the capital stock can be calculated as $C_{90} = I_{90}/\rho$, where $I_{90}$ and $\rho$ is investments made in 1990 and the depreciation rate, respectively. Following King and Fullerton (1984) and Bergman (1997), the depreciation rate for the Swedish industrial firm is set to 0.087. Then, for the year 1991 to 2008, the stock is calculated by applying a perpetual inventory method, i.e., for 1991 the stock is $C_{91} = (1 - 0.087)C_{90} + I_{91}$, and so on. Labor is measured in numbers of workers. Energy is divided into fossil fuel (coal, oil, gaseous fuel), biofuel (wood, heat), and electricity. In Sweden, electricity is an energy carrier that is mainly from hydro, nuclear, and wind power and, therefore, not a significant source of $CO_2$ emissions. Energy is measured in MWh.

Inputs are used to produce one good output, together with emissions of three different air polluters, $CO_2$, $SO_2$, and $NO_x$. $CO_2$ emissions are mainly from using fossil fuels, as biofuels by assumption are carbon neutral. The good output is an index and calculated by dividing the sales value at the firm level by a sector-level producer price index. The emissions are measured in tons. The average annual observation in each of the 14 sectors is displayed in Table 1.1.

Firms within Pulp and Paper, Iron and Steel, and Chemical are the largest energy users. Together they accounted for about 68 percent of total energy consumption in Swedish manufacturing during 1990–2008, more specifically 37.9, 21.3, and 8.7 percent, respectively. Food, Stone and Mineral, Wood, and Mining accounted each for 5 to 6 percent.

Electricity was the most used energy carrier in the industry as a whole. On average, the share of electricity of total energy use in each sector was about 52 percent. Corresponding figures were for fossil fuel and biofuel 38 and 10 percent, respectively (see Figure 1.6). The share of electricity of total energy use was largest in Electro, about 68 percent, Fabricated metal, 67 percent, and Rubber and Plastic, 66 percent. Other sectors with an electricity share larger than 50 percent were Machinery, Motor vehicles, Mining, Pulp and Paper, Chemical, and Printing.

The fossil fuel share of total energy use was the largest in Stone and Mineral, and Iron and Steel, i.e., 78.5 and 69.4 percent, respectively. Other sectors with a share of more than 50 percent were Textile and Food. The largest share of biofuel by far, about 63 percent, is not surprisingly found in Wood. Also, Pulp and Paper exhibits a large share, 21 percent. Excluding these two sectors, the biofuel use of total energy use is on average 5 percent; Machinery (12.7), Electro (9.5), Motor vehicles (9.0), and Printing (7.2) being above average.

The most air polluting sectors are Iron and Steel, Pulp and Paper, and Stone and Mineral, where Iron and Steel in particular stands out. This sector accounted for 30.3, 63.2, and 33.7 percent of total emissions of $CO_2$, $SO_2$, and $NO_x$, respectively, from the manufacturing industry. The corresponding

Table 1.1 Swedish manufacturing industry data, firm level. Descriptive statistics, mean values 1990–2008 (in 2008 prices)

| | N | Capital (MSEK) | Worker | Fossil Fuel (MWh) | Electricity (MWh) | Biofuel (MWh) | Output (index) | $CO_2$ (ton) | $SO_2$ (ton) | $NO_x$ (ton) |
|---|---|---|---|---|---|---|---|---|---|---|
| Mining | 477 | 429 (1551) | 277 (741) | 65969 (242760) | 103872 (343970) | 309 (2768) | 444 (1250) | 20279 (75097) | 25.3 (98.8) | 112.7 (496.9) |
| Food | 4336 | 100 (297) | 201 (506) | 12193 (56092) | 9233 (25781) | 748 (5305) | 391 (1029) | 2978 (13870) | 2.1 (13.6) | 2.7 (14.1) |
| Textile | 1665 | 23 (67) | 71 (131) | 3576 (9629) | 2708 (7856) | 149 (1358) | 57 (87) | 902 (2423) | 0.7 (2.8) | 0.8 (2.2) |
| Wood | 4506 | 46 (128) | 79 (160) | 1160 (5769) | 6262 (15866) | 12543 (35413) | 155 (344) | 314 (1577) | 1.2 (3.6) | 3.8 (9.8) |
| Pulp/Paper | 1624 | 593 (1156) | 427 (775) | 68218 (131060) | 216405 (496640) | 76317 (194147) | 902 (1667) | 18375 (35653) | 29.2 (63) | 39 (81.9) |
| Printing | 1686 | 20 (47) | 67 (105) | 1011 (3574) | 1740 (4076) | 215 (764) | 60 (119) | 248 (898) | 0.1 (1.3) | 0.2 (0.9) |
| Chemical | 1822 | 274 (1230) | 250 (792) | 26725 (101686) | 43782 (144036) | 3503 (20139) | 523 (1930) | 6874 (27663) | 7.6 (45.7) | 6.8 (32) |
| Rubber | 2075 | 41 (94) | 101 (191) | 2211 (6374) | 5002 (9052) | 331 (3409) | 115 (230) | 538 (1450) | 0.3 (1.1) | 0.5 (1.8) |
| Stone | 1878 | 58 (108) | 142 (215) | 37795 (174487) | 9840 (35460) | 487 (2884) | 158 (241) | 11309 (56619) | 6.7 (29.9) | 21.6 (149.5) |

(Continued)

Table 1.1 (Continued)

| | N | Capital (MSEK) | Worker | Fossil Fuel (MWh) | Electricity (MWh) | Biofuel (MWh) | Output (index) | $CO_2$ (ton) | $SO_2$ (ton) | $NO_x$ (ton) |
|---|---|---|---|---|---|---|---|---|---|---|
| Iron/Steel | 666 | 367 (878) | 465 (835) | 344131 (1440698) | 147738 (338657) | 3979 (12073) | 941 (1786) | 63930 (229530) | 282.6 (1360) | 159.1 (721.9) |
| Metal | 2991 | 10 (17) | 42 (134) | 579 (2036) | 1331 (3867) | 88 (497) | 29 (57) | 147 (508) | 0.1 (0.2) | 0.1 (0.5) |
| Machinery | 6252 | 43 (128) | 165 (402) | 1450 (6136) | 3763 (11190) | 759 (4701) | 212 (690) | 366 (1359) | 0.2 (0.9) | 0.3 (1.2) |
| Electro | 2229 | 68 (292) | 324 (1396) | 1475 (5177) | 4547 (14076) | 632 (3004) | 866 (6950) | 392 (1534) | 0.3 (3.6) | 0.3 (1.7) |
| Motor vehicles | 2049 | 382 (1826) | 559 (2090) | 6876 (28814) | 14923 (56427) | 2153 (12152) | 1255 (6295) | 1860 (8229) | 2.4 (16.6) | 1.8 (9) |

Note: standard errors within parenthesis; Rubber = Rubber/Plastic; Stone = Stone/Mineral

figures for Pulp and Paper are 21.2, 15.9, and 20.2, respectively, and for Stone and Mineral, 15.1, 4.2, and 12.9, respectively. To the relatively air polluting sectors can be added Chemical, Food, and Mining. Notable is that the Mining sector accounted for about 17 percent of $NO_x$ emissions in the manufacturing industry as a whole.

Most capital intensive (capital–labor ratio) production is found in the Mining, Pulp and Paper, and Chemical sectors. In these sectors, energy demand is covered up to nearly two-thirds by electricity. Using far the most energy per unit capital is Iron and Steel, but Stone and Mineral also uses more energy-demanding capital compared to the three most capital-intensive sectors. As mentioned above, in Iron and Steel and Stone and Mineral, the demand for energy is covered to nearly 70 and 80 percent, respectively, by fossil fuel. This reliance on fossil fuels depends mainly on reasons related to technology and the production process.

In Figure 1.2, the long-term development of input productivity (output produced over input used) in Swedish manufacturing industry from 1990

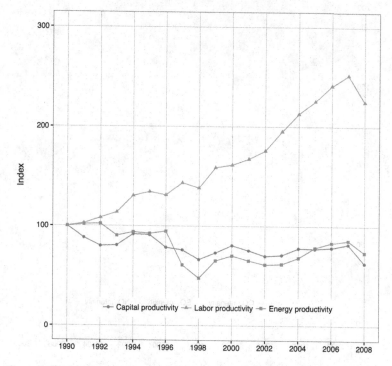

*Figure 1.2* Development of capital productivity (output/capital), labor productivity (output/labor), and energy productivity (output/energy) in Swedish industry between 1990 and 2008. (Index, 1990 = 100)

to 2008 is displayed. It is evident that labor productivity increased substantially. At the same time, the development of capital and energy productivity shows a slightly negative trend. In 2008, the produced output fell sharply due to the global financial crisis. Consequently, we see a sharp decrease in productivity.

Looking at Figure 1.3 and Figure 1.4, as expected, emissions to air vary similarly to energy use in production as shown in Figure 1.2. Increasing energy productivity leads to both lower emissions and reduced emission intensity. Moreover, the negative trend of productivity during the period, i.e., increasing energy use per unit produced output, is reflected by a positive trend of emission levels. However, the link between productivity and emission intensity is not as clear, as shown by the negative trend in $NO_x$ emissions per unit output during the period.

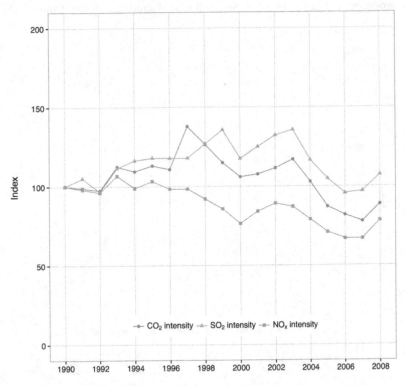

*Figure 1.3* Development of $CO_2$ intensity ($CO_2$/output), $SO_2$ intensity ($SO_2$/output), and $NO_x$ intensity ($NO_x$/output) in Swedish industry between 1990 and 2008. (Index, 1990 = 100)

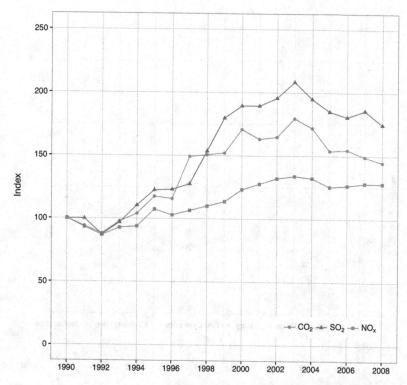

*Figure 1.4* Development of $CO_2$, $SO_2$, and $NO_x$ emissions in Swedish industry between 1990 and 2008. (Index, 1990 = 100)

The large decrease in energy productivity in 1997 and 1998 is accompanied by an increase in emission intensity, except for $NO_x$. Notably, it is only from 1998 onwards that there is a clear negative trend in the development of the $CO_2$ intensity, and it is only from 2005 to 2008 that it is lower than in 1990. $SO_2$ intensity shows a similar development but, in general, the intensity is above the 1990 level.

Capital and labor prices became quite stable during the period, though with opposite trends, as Figure 1.5 shows. The price of capital, calculated as the user cost of capital,[14] halved and the labor price doubled. Starting in the late 1990s and early 2000s, energy prices increased until 2008. In that year the fossil fuel price was more than doubled compared to 1997. The electricity price was about 70 percent higher, and the price of biofuel about 40 to 50 percent higher. It also appears that the price of biofuel was comparatively volatile during the period.

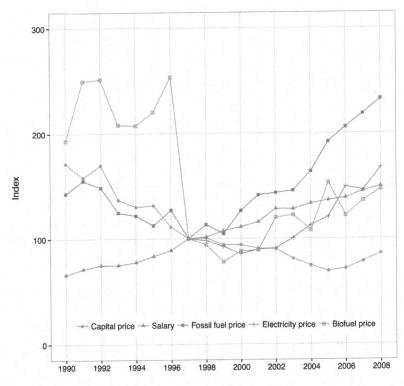

*Figure 1.5* Development of capital price (the user cost of capital), labor price, and energy price in Swedish industry between 1997 and 2008. (Index, 1997 = 100)

Figure 1.5 shows that there is a change in relative prices of energy sources, where the use of fossil fuel becomes more expensive compared to the use of electricity and biofuel. However, as evident from Figure 1.6, the energy mix used in production did not change much during the same period.

Despite a relatively strong increase in the fossil fuel price, the share of fossil fuel was virtually the same in 2008 as in 1990. Instead, it seems that electricity was somewhat substituted for biofuel.

Figure 1.7 reveals the long-term trends in actual energy and $CO_2$ tax rates paid by firms in the Swedish manufacturing industry.

The trends broadly reflect the description of energy and climate policy in Sweden that was provided in Section 1.1. For instance, from 2000 to 2004 the statutory $CO_2$ tax rate was increased by 146 percent. The actual energy tax rate paid fell continuously during 1997–2004, and then the payment began to rise slowly when the manufacturing sector stopped being exempted from energy taxation on electricity use in production. In 2005, the PFE was

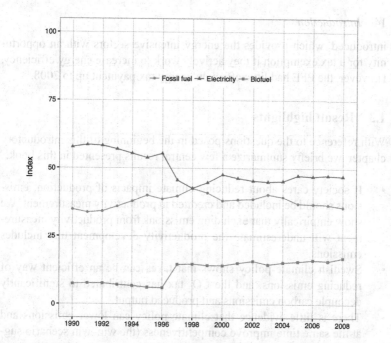

*Figure 1.6* Development of energy mix in Swedish industry between 1990 and 2008

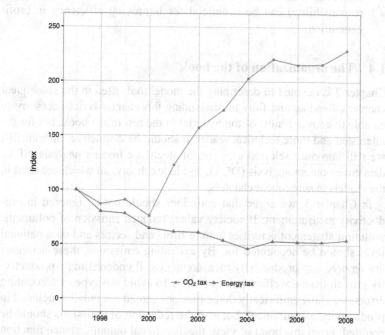

*Figure 1.7* Development of $CO_2$ tax and energy tax in Swedish industry between 1997 and 2008. (Index, 1997 = 100)

introduced, which provides the energy intensive sectors with an opportunity for a tax exemption if they actively work to increase energy efficiency. However, the PFE had little effect on energy tax payment up to 2008.

## 1.3   Result highlights

With reference to the questions posed in the beginning of this introductory chapter, we briefly summarize a few central results presented in this book.

- If society cares about reducing climate impacts of production, emissions should be included and credited in productivity measurement. We show empirically that excluding emissions from productivity measurement will underestimate the productivity development that includes emissions.
- Swedish climate policy shows that taxes can be an efficient way of reducing emissions, and the $CO_2$ tax has contributed to significantly decouple carbon emissions and produced output.
- There is little evidence that climate policy can lower emissions and at the same time improve competitiveness (the win–win scenario suggested by the so-called Porter hypothesis).
- However, it seems that voluntary actions (so-called corporate social responsibility) can be beneficial for improving efficiency in profit generation.

## 1.4   The organization of the book

Chapter 2 is devoted to describing the model tools used in the subsequent chapters. Reading and fully understanding this chapter is not necessary to be able to embrace most of the material in the rest of the book, but for the interested and more technical reader, it should be instructive. Specifically, we will introduce selected elements of stochastic frontier analysis (SFA), data envelopment analysis (DEA), and index theory, all which are used in the models in subsequent chapters.

In Chapter 3, we argue that emissions should not be ignored in productivity measurement. If society values reduced emission of pollutants, pollution abatement activities among firms and sectors and on a national level should be accounted for. By excluding emissions, these activities are ignored and productivity measurement will underestimate productivity growth from a welfare point of view. To avoid this type of accounting errors, we show empirically that emissions should not only be included in productivity measurement, but also the reduction of emissions should be credited. From this point of view, the directional output distance function approach and the Luenberger productivity indicator serve as an appropriate basis.

Since society values reduction of emissions from production, firms are often subject to environmental policy measures. In Chapter 4, we take a closer look at how firms' environmental performance and productivity are affected by climate policy measures. Environmental performance is measured using a carbon intensity index constructed from Shephard's output distance functions. As such, performance is linked to the discussion of decoupling of output production and emissions and the Environmental Kuznets Curve (EKC). Our empirical finding is that the carbon tax has been a significant reason for decoupling in the Swedish manufacturing industry and appears an effective way of lowering carbon emissions. Another finding is that the carbon tax and the EU ETS are policy measures that potentially could put a price on carbon such that firms are spurred to develop technology and improve economic performance in terms of increased productivity. Particularly taking a closer look at the Swedish pulp and paper industry and estimating productivity by applying the Luenberger indicator, the results suggest that the price on carbon faced by this industry through these policy measures has been too low to put pressure on technological development.

In Chapter 5, an SFA approach is adopted to assess the impact of climate policy measures on firms' economic performance. Performance is measured in terms of profit efficiency, here a measure on how efficiently energy inputs are used in production. This is another component of productivity, which is related to how efficient inputs and a given technology are managed, and/or whether the technology used is the best practice or not. We analyze both the direct effect of carbon tax on firms' profit efficiency, and the indirect effect through the effect on firms' environmental performance. In both cases, the empirical analyses show no clear-cut evidence for the so-called Porter hypothesis to be true. That is, the carbon tax has not had an unambiguous positive direct or indirect effect on profit efficiency in the Swedish manufacturing industry. Rather, the result shows that firms' voluntary environmental investments, not driven by the carbon tax, have had a significant positive effect on profit efficiency. This indicates that improved environmental performance may be good for business.

As previously stated, the carbon tax has been restrictive and consequently a significant reason for decoupling in the Swedish manufacturing industry. In Chapter 6, we analyze the unintended consequences of restrictive regulations of emissions in general. We first prove a theorem that explains how regulating emissions may impose bounds on production. Then, inspired by Leif Johansen's capacity framework, we introduce a methodology to empirically rank $CO_2$, $SO_2$, and $NO_x$ emissions with respect to how strongly each of them restricts production due to being subject to regulation. We explicitly measure how much more firms could produce if one air pollutant would be deregulated, compared to the case when all three air pollutants are regulated. The result indicates that the Swedish pulp and paper industry is restricted the most by carbon regulation. Hence, from a pure business point of view, there would be a potential profit gain by deregulating carbon emissions. Regulating carbon emissions also leads to both $SO_2$ and $NO_x$ emissions being reduced, and a policy implication drawn from the result is that relaxing regulation on $NO_x$ may not induce large increases in $NO_x$ emissions. However, it may reduce costs in terms of reduced administrative burden and saved fees.

In Chapter 7, we focus on the firms' perspective. By implementing taxes on emissions, the government burdens firms with tax expenditures that give them incentive to reduce emissions. Here we propose a tool to analyze firms' potential to reduce emissions and, therefore, tax expenditures. The tool is a cost-benefit analysis (CBA) framework, including the cost indirect benefit function and DEA. To demonstrate its practical use, we apply it to Swedish pulp and paper industry data as an example. One insight is that if the government increases emission tax rates, it does not necessarily give firms incentives to implement environmental investments.

## 1.5  Notes

1  See also Brännlund et al. (2014), Lundgren et al. (2015), Lundgren and Marklund (2015), and Lundgren and Marklund (2016) for further details.
2  These tax rates were still valid in 2008.
3  1 EUR ≈ 9.36 SEK in 2015.
4  The tax on energy was at the same time reduced by the corresponding amount.
5  Council Directive (2003/96/EC).
6  Swedish Energy Agency website, http://www.energimyndigheten.se/en/ sustainability/companies-and-businesses/the-programme-for-improving-energy-efficiency-in-energy-intensive-industries/results-of-the-first-five-years-in-pfe/, 2016-01-27.
7  Swedish Energy Agency website, http://www.energimyndigheten.se/energi effektivisering/program-och-uppdrag/avslutade-program/pfe/, 2016-01-27.
8  Notably, as the first country ever, Australia abolished the $CO_2$ tax in 2014 (Australian Government, Department of the Environment, https://www.environment. gov.au/climate-change/repealing-carbon-tax, 2016-01-18).
9  See the European Commission website, http://ec.europa.eu/clima/policies/ets/ index_en.htm.
10  Governed by the Directive 2003/87/EC, and amended by Directive 2004/101/EC.
11  In 2012, aviation also came to be covered by the EU ETS.
12  The ongoing third period of trade is running until 2020. Additional sectors are covered by the trade and a difference is now that the cap of allowances is set at the EU level. Also, an increasing proportion of allowances will be auctioned among the emission sources. Today, EU ETS covers 45 percent of total greenhouse gas emissions among the EU Member States.

13 We obtained the data of carbon market price from www.bluenext.eu in early 2012. Last access to the website was in October 2013. However, at present, it is shut down for unknown reasons.

14 The user cost of capital is calculated as $c_t = I_t(r_t + \delta)$, where $I_t$ is investment in capital in year t, $r_t$ is the interest rate, and $\delta$ is the depreciation rate. As in the case of constructing the capital stock, the depreciation rate is set to 0.087.

## 1.6 References

Bergman, M., 1997. The Restricted Profit Function and the Application of the Generalized Leontief and the Translog Functional Forms. *International Journal of Production Economics* 49(3): 245–254.

Blomberg, J., E. Henriksson, R. Lundmark, 2012. Energy Efficiency and Policy in Swedish Pulp and Paper Mills: A Data Envelope Analysis Approach. *Energy Policy* 42: 569–579.

Brännlund, R., 2009. The Tax System's Options and Tasks within Environmental Policy. In Bolandern J. (ed.), *The Non-Fiscal Purposes of Taxation*: 187–212. Yearbook for Nordic Tax Research 2009, DJØF Publishing Copenhagen, Denmark.

Brännlund, R., T. Lundgren, P-O. Marklund, 2014. Carbon Intensity in Production and the Effects of Climate Policy – Evidence from Swedish Industry. *Energy Policy* 67: 844–857.

Council Directive 2003/96/EC of 27 October, 2003. Restructuring the Community Framework for the Taxation of Energy Products and Electricity.

King, M.A., D. Fullerton, 1984. *The Taxation of Income from Capital: A Comparative Study of the United States, the United Kingdom, Sweden and West Germany*. The University of Chicago Press, Chicago and London.

Lundgren, T., P-O. Marklund, 2015. Climate Policy, Environmental Performance, and Profits. *Journal of Productivity Analysis* 44(3): 225–235.

Lundgren, T., P-O. Marklund, 2016. An Analysis of the Swedish $CO_2$ Tax and Its Impact on Firm Performance. WP 2016: 1, Centre for Environmental and Resource Economics (www.cere.se/en).

Lundgren, T., P-O. Marklund, E. Samakovlis, W. Zhou, 2015. Carbon Prices and Incentives for Technological Development. *Journal of Environmental Management* 150: 393–403.

Mansikkasalo, A., P. Söderholm, 2013. Voluntary Agreements for Industrial Energy Use: Self-selection and Electricity Savings in the Swedish PFE Program. In Mansikkasalo, A., 2013. Greening Industry: Essays on Industrial Energy Use and Markets for Forest Raw Material (Ph.D Thesis), Department of Economics, Luleå University of Technology.

OECD, 2013. Taxing Energy Use: A Graphical Analysis. OECD Publishing. http://dx.doi.org/10.1787/9789264183933-en.

Palmer, K., W.E. Oates, P.P. Portney, 1995. Tightening Environmental Standards: The Benefit-Cost or the No-Cost Paradigm? *Journal of Economic Perspectives* 9(4): 119–132.

Porter, M.E., C. van der Linde, 1995. Toward a New Conception of the Environmental-Competitiveness Relationship. *Journal of Economic Perspectives* 9(4): 97–118.

Statistics Sweden, 2000. Environmental Taxes and Environmentally Damaging Subsidies. Statistics Sweden (SCB), Report 2000: 3.

Swedish Energy Agency, 2006. Ekonomiska Styrmedel i Energisektorn: En Utvärdering av dess Effekter på Koldioxidutsläppen från 1990. Swedish Energy Agency, ER 2006: 6 (in Swedish).

Swedish Energy Agency, 2008. Energiläget 2008. Energimyndigheten, ER2008: 15 (in Swedish).

Swedish Energy Agency, 2010. Energy in Sweden 2010. The Swedish Energy Agency.

Swedish Environmental Protection Agency, 2003. Kväveoxidavgiften – Ett Effektivt Styrmedel (Reducing NOx Emissions – An Evaluation of the Nitrogen Oxide Charge). Naturvårdesverket, Rapport 5335, November 2003 (in Swedish; Extended summary in English).

Swedish National Audit Office, 2012. Klimatrelaterade Skatter – Vem Betalar? RIR 2012: 1 (in Swedish).

# 2 Method and models

In this chapter, we introduce a set of models that are used in the book. In particular, the models are used to assess the performance of the Swedish industry with respect to environmental policy. We provide a uniform and integrated overview, and the chapter may be read as a self-contained set of production models when some outputs are undesirable byproducts. The chapter provides a background to the rest of the book.

## 2.1 Models of technology in terms of sets, including goods and bads

Next, we introduce the technology and production models that are used in the various applications in the book. We start by thinking of technology as a set of inputs and outputs, and formalize this by introducing axioms intended to reflect basic physical realities of production. They are consistent with measuring economic performance, especially in the case when good outputs are jointly produced with undesirable outputs. We focus on sets with multiple inputs and outputs, including what we normally think of as production possibilities set, total product set, and input sets.

We begin with the production set, which models inputs transformed into outputs via a general production process, which at this point we refer to as the black box. More formally, we model the black box transforming input vectors $x \in \Re_+^N$ into output vectors $y \in \Re_+^M$. At this point, the black box – the production process – is not specified as specific sub-processes – we discuss more sophisticated models with good and bad outputs including abatement sub-technologies later in this section.

The black box technology $T$ is defined as

$$T = \{(x, y) : x \text{ can produce } y\}. \tag{2.1}$$

If we further simplify to the case of a single input producing a single output, we may graph $T$ as in Figure 2.2. The boundary of this set is often

*Figure 2.1* A black box technology

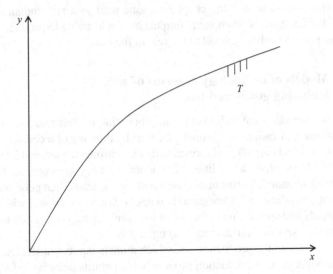

*Figure 2.2* The technology set *T*

referred to as the total product curve and reflects the notion that increasing input can lead to increased output.

We can also look at the underlying technology in two alternative ways – in terms of the output sets $P(x)$ and the input sets $L(y)$.

$$P(x) = \{y : (x, y) \in T\}, x \in \Re_+^N \qquad (2.2)$$

$$L(y) = \{x : (x, y) \in T\}, y \in \Re_+^M. \qquad (2.3)$$

These three set representations of technology are equivalently related by

$$x \in L(y) \Leftrightarrow (x, y) \in T \Leftrightarrow y \in P(x). \tag{2.4}$$

For these equivalent representations to hold, no particular assumptions on the technology are required. However, to think of these as representing a feasible production technology, we impose some minimal conditions.[1] Following Shephard (1970) we impose the following standard assumptions:

$P(0) = 0$, which allows for inactivity and implies that zero input cannot produce positive output.

$P(x)$ is bounded for all $x \in \Re_+^N$, which imposes scarcity.

$P(x') \supseteq P(x)$, when $x' \geq x$, free disposability of inputs, which allows for wasted inputs.

$y \in P(x), 0 \leq \lambda \leq 1 \Rightarrow \lambda y \in P(x)$, weak disposability of outputs, which – when they are produced – models costly reduction of bads.

$P(x)$ is closed and nonempty for all $x \in \Re_+^N$.

We note that scarcity and closedness imply that the output set $P(x)$ is compact for all $x \in \Re_+^N$, which will prove useful when measuring performance.

This book is mainly concerned with technologies that produce undesirable (bad) outputs as well as the good or intended outputs $y \in \Re_+^M$. In this case, we may augment the simple black box to include a bad output vector $b \in \Re_+^J$ (see Figure 2.3).

In this case, the technology produces $b \in \Re_+^J$ in addition to $y \in \Re_+^M$. Baumgärtner et al. (2001, p. 365) note the connection of this type of technology to thermodynamics

. . . the production of wanted goods gives rise to additional unwanted outputs . . .

*Figure 2.3* A black box with bads

Shephard and Färe (1974) formalize this idea of production with unwanted byproducts with their notion of null-joint production:

If $(y,b) \in P(x)$ and $b = 0$ then $y = 0$. (2.5)

Here the technology is augmented to include bad outputs, i.e.,

$$P(x) = \{(y,b) : x \text{ can produce } y,b\}, x \in \Re_+^N.$$ (2.6)

This says that if goods and bads are null-joint, then if any good output is produced, then there must be some bad outputs produced as byproducts, or "no fire without smoke".[2]

In addition to $y$ and $b$ being null-joint, we may also assume that they are jointly weakly disposable:

$$(y,b) \in P(x) \text{ and } 0 \leq \lambda \leq 1 \text{ then } (\lambda y, \lambda b) \in P(x)$$ (2.7)

and that good output is freely or strongly disposable:[3]

$$(y,b) \in P(x), y' \leq y \Rightarrow (y',b) \in P(x).$$ (2.8)

An output set with inputs $x$ producing one desirable and one undesirable output satisfying the conditions of null-joint production, joint weak disposability of good and bad output and strong disposability of good output is illustrated below.

If $y$ and $b$ are null-joint and $b = 0$, then for $(y,b)$ to be feasible, i.e., $(y,b) \in P(x)$, it must be true that $y = 0$ since zero bad output implies zero good output in this case. Put differently, for good output $y$ to be positive then bad output $b$ must also be positive. In our figure, this implies that production can occur on the $y$-axis only at the origin. Figure 2.4 also illustrates the joint weak disposability of $(y,b)$, if $(y,b)$ is feasible so are proportional contractions, i.e., $(\lambda y, \lambda b) \in P(x)$ for all $\lambda, 0 \leq \lambda \leq 1$.

This model, in particular the assumption of weak disposability of $(y,b)$, has been challenged by Førsund (2009) and Murty et al. (2012), which we address below.

To justify our assumption of joint weak disposability of good and bad output, we go inside our augmented black box. Following Färe et al. (2013), consider the joint production of electricity and $SO_2$. This production process consists of two "sub-technologies" – electricity production $P^1(x^1)$ and an abatement sub-technology $P^2(x^2,b)$, which we illustrate in Figure 2.5.

The two sub-technologies share inputs so that

$$x^1 + x^2 = x,$$ (2.9)

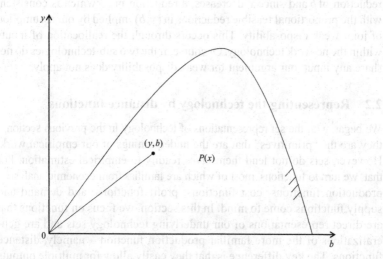

*Figure 2.4* Null-joint weakly disposable technology

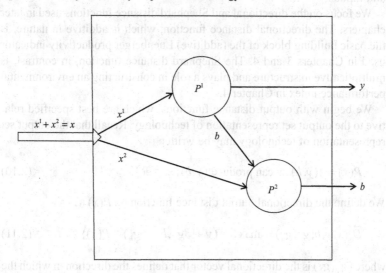

*Figure 2.5* Network with abatement

where $x$ is the total amount of inputs available. $P^1(x^1)$ produces $y$ with byproduct $b$, and then $b$ becomes an input into the abatement technology $P^2(x^2,b)$, where inputs $x^2$ are applied to reduce $b$. We call this a network technology.

To reduce the final output of bads, one may reallocate more $x$ to $P^2$, which requires reducing $x^1$, and therefore $y$. Thus, we have that more $x^2$ leads to a reduction of $b$ and since $x^1$ decreases, a reduction in $y$, which is consistent with the proportional feasible reductions in $(y,b)$ implied by our assumption of joint weak disposability. This occurs through the reallocation of inputs within the network technology. Of course, if the two sub-technologies do not share any input, our argument for weak disposability does not apply.

## 2.2   Representing the technology by distance functions

We began with the set representations of technology in the previous section – they are the "primitives" that are the underpinnings of our empirical work. However, sets do not lend themselves readily to empirical estimation. For that, we turn to functions, most of which are familiar from economic analysis – production functions, cost functions, profit functions, and demand and supply functions come to mind. In this section, we focus on functions that are direct representations of our underlying technology sets and are generalizations of the more familiar production function – namely, distance functions. The key difference is that they easily allow for multiple outputs and inputs.

We focus on the directional and Shephard distance functions used in later chapters. The directional distance function, which is additive in nature, is the basic building block of the (additive) Luenberger productivity indicator used in Chapters 3 and 4. The Shephard distance function, in contrast, is multiplicative in structure and plays a role in constructing an environmental performance index in Chapter 4.

We begin with output distance functions, which are best specified relative to the output set representation of technology. Recall that the output set representation of technology may be written

$$P(x) = \{(y,b) : x \text{ can produce } (y,b)\}, x \in \Re_+^N. \tag{2.10}$$

We define the directional output distance function on $P(x)$ as

$$\vec{D}_o(x,y,b;g_y,g_b) = \max\{\beta : (y + \beta g_y, b - \beta g_b) \in P(x)\} \tag{2.11}$$

where $(g_y, g_b)$ is the directional vector that defines the direction in which the output vector $(y,b)$ is projected toward the frontier (boundary) of the output set. We illustrate in Figure 2.6, assuming that good and bad outputs are null-joint and jointly weakly disposable, and $y$ strongly disposable.

The technology is given by $P(x)$ and the directional vector $g = (g_y, -g_b)$ is such that good output is expanded while bad output is contracted, consistent with the environmental policy goals we model in the following chapters. The directional distance function projects $(y,b)$ in the direction $g = (g_y, -g_b)$

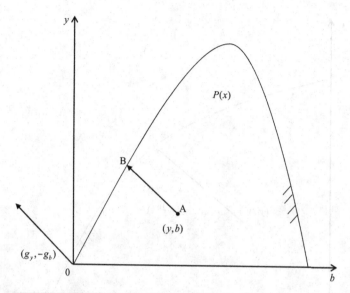

*Figure 2.6* The directional output distance function

until $(y+\beta g_y, b-\beta g_b)$ reaches the boundary of $P(x)$, i.e., it takes $(y,b)$ from A to B in the figure. Here production at A is inefficient, which results in the value of the directional distance function that is greater than zero. Production at B is efficient and $\vec{D}_o(x^B, y^B, b^B; g)=0$: it is not possible to increase good output and contract bad output at B and still remain within $P(x)$.

If we also assume that the technology satisfies directional disposability

$$(y,b) \in P(x), 0 \leqq \lambda \leqq 1, \text{ then } (y+\lambda g_y, b-\lambda g_b) \in P(x), \qquad (2.12)$$

then the distance function completely represents technology in the sense that

$$\vec{D}_o(x,y,b; g_y, g_b) \geqq 0 \Leftrightarrow (y,b) \in P(x), \qquad (2.13)$$

which means that every feasible member of the technology can be equivalently represented by this distance function.

Now we turn to Shephard distance functions, which can be derived as a special case of the directional distance functions. Starting with the Shephard's output distance function (Shephard, 1970), we assume the simple case in which there are no bad outputs, i.e., where the output set is defined as

$$P(x) = \{y : x \text{ can produce } y\}, x \in \Re_+^N, \qquad (2.14)$$

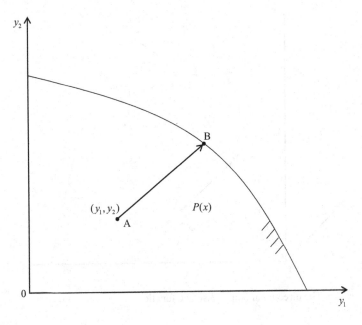

*Figure 2.7* Shephard's output distance function

and the Shephard's output distance function is defined as

$$D_o(x,y) = \min\{\lambda : y / \lambda \in P(x)\}. \tag{2.15}$$

This function expands output vector $y$ proportionally (i.e., on a ray from the origin through the point under evaluation) as much as possible while remaining an element of the output set. Figure 2.7 illustrates.

The output set $P(x)$ with no bad output but multiple good outputs in the figure satisfies free disposability of outputs, i.e.,

$$y \in P(x) \text{ and } y' \leq y \Rightarrow y' \in P(x), \tag{2.16}$$

which means that with the given inputs $x$, although maximum feasible outputs maybe achieved (those on the boundary of the set), a firm could "waste" or freely dispose of some or all of these by moving to southwest in the technology.

In our figure, the distance function expands $(y_1, y_2)$ from A to B, and B is on the boundary or frontier of $P(x)$. Production is inefficient at A, since with the inputs $x$, output at B is feasible, and $D_o(x, y^A) < 1$. Taking $1 / D_o(x, y^A)$

gives the percentage by which outputs could be increased proportionally if A were efficient. Production at B on the other hand is efficient and $D_o(x, y^B) = 1$. It is not possible to further expand output at B and remain in $P(x)$.

Since outputs are freely disposable

$$D_o(x, y) \leq 1 \Leftrightarrow y \in P(x), \tag{2.17}$$

i.e., the distance function completely represents the underlying output set.[4]

We can now show the relationship between the directional output distance function and the Shephard's output distance function. For this simple case with no undesirable outputs, the directional output distance function is defined as

$$\vec{D}_o(x, y; g_y) = \max\{\beta : (y + \beta g_y) \in P(x)\}. \tag{2.18}$$

If in addition we choose the direction vector $g_y$ to be the observed data $y$, the directional distance function may be written

$$\begin{aligned} \vec{D}_o(x, y; y) &= \max\{\beta : (y + \beta y) \in P(x)\} \\ &= \max\{\beta : y(1 + \beta) \in P(x)\} \end{aligned} \tag{2.19}$$

and if we take $(1 + \beta) = \lambda$ above, then the Shephard distance function (which scales in the direction $y$) is a special case of the more general directional distance function, namely

$$\vec{D}_o(x, y; y) = (1 / D_o(x, y)) - 1. \tag{2.20}$$

Efficiency under the directional distance function yields a value of zero, whereas the Shephard distance function value would be one.

We may also define distance functions in terms of input efficiency. Shephard (1953)'s input distance function mimics his output distance function in being multiplicative in nature. It is defined relative to the input set $L(y)$ rather than the output set, but represents the same underlying technology:

$$x \in L(y) \Leftrightarrow y \in P(x). \tag{2.21}$$

It is defined as

$$D_i(y, x) = \max\{\lambda : x / \lambda \in L(y)\}, y \in \Re_+^M, \tag{2.22}$$

and we illustrate it in Figure 2.8.

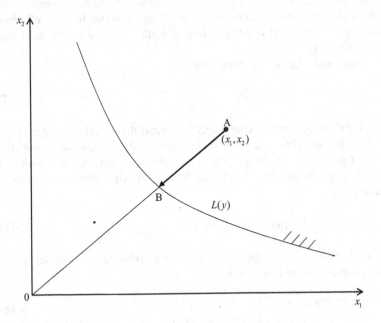

*Figure 2.8* Shephard's input distance function

Technology is represented by the input set, $L(y), y \in \Re_+^M$, where inputs are freely disposable:

$$x' \geq x \in L(y) \Rightarrow x' \in L(y). \tag{2.23}$$

The input vector $(x_1, x_2)$ is projected (contracted) onto the boundary of $L(y)$, thus the distance function takes $(x_1, x_2)$ from A to B, signaling technical inefficiency or $D_i(y, x) > 1$. And since inputs are freely disposable, the Shephard input distance function completely represents technology in the sense that

$$D_i(y, x) \geq 1 \Leftrightarrow x \in L(y). \tag{2.24}$$

One can also prove that under constant returns to scale, Shephard's distance functions are reciprocals,

$$D_o(x, y) = 1 / D_i(y, x). \tag{2.25}$$

We employ both Shephard input and output distance functions to construct our environmental performance indices in Chapter 4. We estimate these using DEA, to which we turn in the next section.

## 2.3 Formulating technology in terms of (nonparametric) data envelopment analysis

We now turn to nonparametric specification of our representations of technology. The DEA or nonparametric approach allows us to formulate the underlying set technology as a system of inequalities, which can then be combined with an objective function to estimate our distance (and profit) functions as solutions to simple linear programming problems without requiring specification of particular functional forms.

We begin here with the simple case with no undesirable outputs, after which we augment the technology to include bads. Our data consist of $k = 1,\ldots,K$ observations or firms that are referred to in the DEA literature as decision making units (DMUs). Each DMU employs $x_k \in \Re_+^N$ inputs to produce $y_k \in \Re_+^M$ outputs. This may be represented as a matrix:

| DMU | 1 | 2 | $\cdots$ | K |
|---|---|---|---|---|
| **Inputs** 1 | $x_{11}$ | $x_{21}$ | $\cdots$ | $x_{K1}$ |
| 2 | $x_{12}$ | $x_{22}$ | $\cdots$ | $x_{K2}$ |
| $\vdots$ | $\vdots$ | $\vdots$ | $\vdots$ | $\vdots$ |
| N | $x_{1N}$ | $x_{2N}$ | $\cdots$ | $x_{KN}$ |
| **Outputs** 1 | $y_{11}$ | $y_{21}$ | $\cdots$ | $y_{K1}$ |
| 2 | $y_{12}$ | $y_{22}$ | $\cdots$ | $y_{K2}$ |
| $\vdots$ | $\vdots$ | $\vdots$ | $\vdots$ | $\vdots$ |
| M | $y_{1M}$ | $y_{2M}$ | $\cdots$ | $y_{KM}$ |

where each column is a DMU and each row is an input or an output.

In the original DEA model by Charnes et al. (1978), each input and output was required to be strictly positive. Here we follow Kemeny et al. (1956) and assume that the following less restrictive conditions hold:

$$\sum_{m=1}^{M} y_{km} > 0, k = 1,\ldots,K, \quad \sum_{k=1}^{K} y_{km} > 0, m = 1,\ldots,M, \quad (2.26)$$

$$\sum_{n=1}^{N} x_{kn} > 0, k = 1,\ldots,K, \quad \sum_{k=1}^{K} x_{kn} > 0, n = 1,\ldots,N.$$

These conditions, which were introduced to generalize the von Neumann (1945) assumptions of strict positivity, state that each input and output matrix must have at least one nonzero element in each row and column. These conditions also ensure that the DEA technology satisfies the conditions of inactivity and compactness that we introduced earlier on the output set. In order to impose further assumptions, we construct the DEA technology that uses the data from the input and output matrices introduced above as well as intensity variables $z$ (to be discussed in some detail presently) which describes $P(x)$ as the following set of inequalities

$$P(x^{k'}) = \{y : \sum_{k=1}^{K} z_k y_{km} \geq y_m, m = 1, \ldots, M,$$

$$\sum_{k=1}^{K} z_k x_{kn} \leq x_{k'n}, n = 1, \ldots, N, \tag{2.27}$$

$$z_k \geq 0, k = 1, \ldots, K\}.$$

From the definition of the output set, we know that it is the set of all feasible outputs $y$ that the given input bundle $x$ can produce given available technology. Here the "given" inputs are those observed in our sample as in the array above. In particular, our actual data are included in the left-hand side of the inequalities and denoted with a subscript $k$. The right-hand side represents the hypothetical data that do NOT have a subscript $k$ here, since these are variables that we created to "complete" or fill in the technology. At the same time, all of the data – observed or constructed – must satisfy our assumptions concerning disposability, etc., in Section 2.1. The intensity variables, $z_k$, are associated with the individual DMUs, $k = 1, \ldots, K$. Here they serve as "dot-connectors", i.e., they serve to provide linear combinations (weighted averages) of the data in the sample, which become part of the reference output set.

The inequalities $\leq$ and $\geq$ in the input and output constraints (respectively) ensure that they satisfy free disposability. Thus in the output constraints, the weighted average of the observed data (left-hand side) must be $\geq$ the "hypothetical" data on the right-hand side, i.e., the hypothetical data can be less efficient than the observed data, which is what we mean by free disposability of outputs. The inequality is reversed in the input constraints, since free disposability of inputs means that we may waste additional inputs.

Since the intensity variables $z_k, k = 1, \ldots, K$ are only required to be nonnegative, the technology satisfies constant returns to scale (CRS), which for the output set implies

$$P(\lambda x) = \lambda P(x), \lambda \geq 0. \tag{2.28}$$

Finally, by further restricting the intensity variables, alternative returns to scale may be imposed:

(a)   $\sum_{k=1}^{K} z_k \leq 1, z_k \geq 0, k = 1, \ldots, K$   Nonincreasing Returns to Scale,

(b) $\sum_{k=1}^{K} z_k = 1, z_k \geq 0, k = 1,\ldots,K$   Variable Returns to Scale.

Next, we augment the data matrix to include undesirable or bad outputs:

| DMU | | 1 | 2 | ... | K |
|-----|---|-----|-----|-----|-----|
| Bads | 1 | $b_{11}$ | $b_{21}$ | ... | $b_{K1}$ |
| | 2 | $b_{12}$ | $b_{22}$ | ... | $b_{K2}$ |
| | ⋮ | ⋮ | ⋮ | ⋮ | ⋮ |
| | J | $b_{1J}$ | $b_{2J}$ | ... | $b_{KJ}$ |

With this amendment, the DEA output set with goods and bads becomes

$$P(x^{k'}) = \{(y,b): \sum_{k=1}^{K} z_k y_{km} \geq y_m, m = 1,\ldots,M,$$

$$\sum_{k=1}^{K} z_k b_{kj} = b_j, j = 1,\ldots,J, \tag{2.29}$$

$$\sum_{k=1}^{K} z_k x_{kn} \leq x_{k'n}, n = 1,\ldots,N,$$

$$z_k \geq 0, k = 1,\ldots,K\}.$$

Each of the good output constraints, $m = 1,\ldots,M$ again have the "$\geq$" type constraints, implying that these good outputs are strongly disposable. The constraints for the bad outputs, $j = 1,\ldots,J$ are strict equalities, with the result that the good and bad outputs are jointly weakly disposable as discussed in Section 2.1.[5] To introduce null-jointness between the good and bad outputs, we require that the bad data matrix includes one strictly positive component in each row and column, i.e.,

DMU

$$\sum_{j=1}^{J} b_{kj} > 0, k = 1,\ldots,K,$$

$$\sum_{k=1}^{K} b_{kj} > 0, j = 1,\ldots,J, \tag{2.30}$$

If all of the right-hand side variables $b_j, j = 1,\ldots,J$ are zero in the augmented $P(x)$ technology, then all $z_k, k = 1,\ldots,K$ must also be zero, therefore, $y_m = 0, m = 1,\ldots,M$ as well. These conditions may be altered so that individual or groups of $b$:s may be null-joint with the $b$:s.

We illustrate the output set $P(x)$ constructed using DEA and satisfying weak disposability of good and bad outputs and null-jointness in Figure 2.9 below.

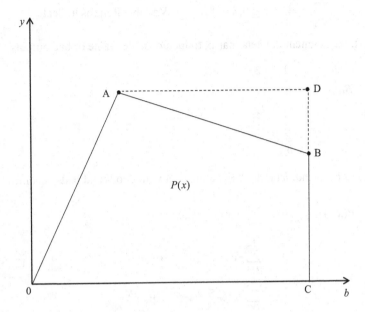

*Figure 2.9* An output set with good and bad outputs

Here inputs $x$ produce good and bad outputs. Suppose we have two observations A and B; the resulting output set using DEA satisfies the following weak disposability constraint for these data:

$$z_A b_A + z_B b_B = b \tag{2.31}$$

which results in the output set being bounded by 0ABC0. In this case, both A and B would be considered "efficient" in the sense that they are on the boundary of the set.[6] The downward slope of segment AB suggests that observation B could (using their current outputs $x$) move along the segment and simultaneously increase good output and decrease bad output, which suggests that B is not efficient in a Pareto sense. One way this situation could be avoided is to extend the output set to include the counterfactual point D, which would extend the output set boundary to 0ADC0, see Färe et al. (2014). This condition is obtained by introducing an inequality constraint ($\leqq$) so that

$$z_A b_A + z_B b_B \leqq b. \tag{2.32}$$

In order to maintain scarcity, an upper bound on the bad output may be added as well.

To sum up, we have created a DEA model of technology $P(x)$ with good and bad outputs that satisfies the "environmental" assumptions that $y$ and $b$ are jointly weakly disposable and that $y$ and $b$ are null-joint. These technologies are employed in Chapters 3, 4, 6, and 7.

## 2.4 Estimating performance with nonparametric and parametric forms

In this book, we measure performance in a number of ways, including relative to maximum profit (by estimating a profit function) or estimating technical efficiency and environmental efficiency or productivity using directional and Shephard's distance functions. Intuitively, we are now thinking about adding an objective function to our production technologies. We can then estimate performance either by using the nonparametric specification of technology from the previous section or by taking a parametric/econometric approach requiring specification of a functional form. We begin with our nonparametric models and their formulation and estimation.

The distance functions we specified in Section 2.2 were static in nature. Another type of nonparametric performance measure employed here using distance functions focuses on the technology and how it changes over time, namely productivity growth, especially productivity when some outputs are undesirable as in Chapters 3 and 4. There we use the Luenberger productivity indicator introduced by Chambers (1996), which can accommodate good and bad outputs, is nonparametric, and does not require price data. This indicator is defined in terms of the directional output distance function introduced earlier in this chapter. The Luenberger productivity indicator that explicitly includes bad outputs is defined as

$$L_t^{t+1}(x,y,b;g_y,g_b) = 1/2[\vec{D}_o^{t+1}(x^t,y^t,b^t;g_y,g_b) - \vec{D}_o^{t+1}(x^{t+1},y^{t+1},b^{t+1};g_y,g_b) \atop + \vec{D}_o^t(x^t,y^t,b^t;g_y,g_b) - \vec{D}_o^t(x^{t+1},y^{t+1},b^{t+1};g_y,g_b)], \quad (2.33)$$

where $\vec{D}_o^\tau$ is the reference technology constructed from $\tau(\tau = t, t+1)$ data and $(x^\tau, y^\tau, b^\tau)$ are the corresponding input and output data.

Chambers et al. (1996) show that the Luenberger productivity indicator may also be decomposed into an efficiency change $LECH_t^{t+1}$ and a technical change component $LTCH_t^{t+1}$, where

$$LECH_t^{t+1} = \vec{D}_o^t(x^t,y^t,b^t;g_y,g_b) - \vec{D}_o^{t+1}(x^{t+1},y^{t+1},b^{t+1};g_y,g_b) \quad (2.34)$$

and

$$LTCH_t^{t+1} = 1/2[\vec{D}_o^{t+1}(x^{t+1},y^{t+1},b^{t+1};g_y,g_b) - \vec{D}_o^t(x^{t+1},y^{t+1},b^{t+1};g_y,g_b) \atop + \vec{D}_o^{t+1}(x^t,y^t,b^t;g_y,g_b) + \vec{D}_o^t(x^t,y^t,b^t;g_y,g_b)]. \quad (2.35)$$

$LECH_t^{t+1}$ is a measure of catching up to the frontier of $P(x)$ between adjacent periods and $LTCH_t^{t+1}$ measures the shifts in the frontier between adjacent periods.

Estimation of a typical component directional distance function with bads in period implements the (time-augmented) definition:

$$\vec{D}_o^\tau(x^\tau, y^\tau, b^\tau; g_y, g_b) = \max\{\beta : (y^\tau + \beta g_y, b^\tau - \beta g_b) \in P(x)\}. \quad (2.36)$$

This is achieved by adding the objective to the (time-augmented) DEA technology specified in the previous section, and estimating the resulting linear programming problems for each observation in the sample, $k' = 1, \ldots, K$:

$$\vec{D}_o^\tau(x_{k'}^\tau, y_{k'}^\tau, b_{k'}^\tau; g_y, g_b) = \max \quad \beta$$

$$s.t. \quad \sum_{k=1}^{K} z_k y_{km}^\tau \geq y_{k'm}^\tau + \beta g_y, \, m = 1, \ldots, M,$$

$$\sum_{k=1}^{K} z_k b_{kj}^\tau = b_{k'j}^\tau - \beta g_b, \, j = 1, \ldots, J, \quad (2.37)$$

$$\sum_{k=1}^{K} z_k x_{kn}^\tau \leq x_{k'n}^\tau, \, n = 1, \ldots, N,$$

$$z_k \geq 0, \, k = 1, \ldots, K.$$

Note that now the right-hand side of the constraints specifies an individual DMU ($K'$) under evaluation rather than our hypothetical data from earlier and includes the $\beta g$ terms. In addition, the $\tau$ time superscripts can take alternative values $\tau = t, t+1$, as required. In particular, the data on the right-hand side and left-hand side of the inequality constraints may be from two different periods, allowing for comparing data from one period to another.

Returning to our Shephard's distance functions, in Chapter 4 we make use of the environmental performance index introduced by Färe et al. (1999), which is constructed from Shephard distance functions. The index is the ratio of two Malmquist (1953) quantity indexes, one for good outputs and one for bads. Both quantity indexes are ratios of distance functions, which is what Malmquist used to define his consumer quantity indexes.

To motivate the index, we begin by thinking of the case of a single good and a single bad output in situations $k$ and $l$:

$$E^{k,l} = \frac{y^l / b^l}{y^k / b^k} = \frac{y^l / y^k}{b^l / b^k}, \quad (2.38)$$

where the first set of ratios compare two average good/bad productivities and the second set of ratios are a "good" quantity index divided by a "bad" quantity index. This is simple to compute if there is only one bad and one good; however, in the more general case where there may be multiple goods and bads, we need the help of our distance functions, which readily allow for multiple outputs and inputs.

To formulate our Malmquist good and bad quantity indexes, we need to introduce what we call subvector distance functions:

$$D_y(x,y,b) = \min\{\theta : (y/\theta,b) \in P(x)\} \tag{2.39}$$

and

$$D_b(x,y,b) = \max\{\theta : (y,b/\theta) \in P(x)\}. \tag{2.40}$$

The first of these is a subvector output distance function in which we want to expand good output and the second is a subvector input distance function where we want to contract bad output. Both distance function are homogeneous of degree +1 in the scaled output subvector, e.g., $D_y(x,1 \cdot y,b) = yD_y(x,1,b)$.

Introducing these distance functions to our index, we have

$$
\begin{aligned}
E^{k,l} &= \frac{y^l/y^k}{b^l/b^k} = \left(\frac{y^l D_y(x^o,1,b^o)}{y^k D_y(x^o,1,b^o)}\right) \Bigg/ \left(\frac{b^l D_b(x^o,y^o,1)}{b^k D_b(x^o,y^o,1)}\right) \\
&= \frac{D_y(x^o,y^l,b^o)/D_y(x^o,y^k,b^o)}{D_b(x^o,y^o,b^l)/D_b(x^o,y^o,b^k)},
\end{aligned}
\tag{2.41}
$$

where $D_y(x^o,y^l,b^o)/D_y(x^o,y^k,b^o) = Q_y$ is a good output quantity index and $D_b(x^o,y^o,b^l)/D_b(x^o,y^o,b^k) = Q_b$ is a bad quantity index. The superscript $o$ indicates a reference or normalization vector. Thus, our environmental index can accommodate multiple bads and goods and can be used, for example, to track whether individual firms are improving their ratio of good to bad output over time or relative to other firms, given a reference or hypothetical firm (see Chapter 4).

Next, we turn to our performance estimation employing parametric functional forms. The function we estimate parametrically in this book is the profit function. We start with the simple case and assume that we are given input and output prices $(w,p)$ and a technology set $T$, which for the moment does not include bad outputs, i.e.,

$$T = \{(x,y) : x \text{ can produce } y\} \tag{2.42}$$

and the (maximum) profit function[7] is defined as

$$\pi(p,w) = \max_{y,x}\{py - wx : (x,y) \in T\} \tag{2.43}$$

which we illustrate in Figure 2.10.

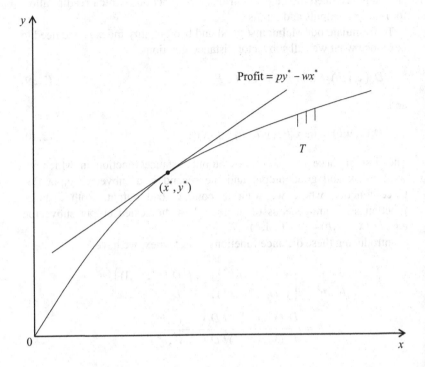

*Figure 2.10* Profit maximization

In the figure, the technology $T$ is the set below and including the curved line and profit ($py - wx$) reaches its maximum at $(x^*, y^*)$,

$$\pi(p,w) = py^* - wx^*. \tag{2.44}$$

We note that the profit function is homogeneous of degree +1 in prices, i.e.,

$$\pi(\lambda p, \lambda w) = \lambda py - \lambda wx = \lambda \Pi(p,w), \lambda > 0. \tag{2.45}$$

## 2.5    Profit efficiency: stochastic frontier analysis

The profit efficiency approach adopted in Chapter 5 in this book is based on Kumbhakar and Lovell (2000) and Kumbhakar (2001). The approach measures the percentage loss in profits due to technical inefficiency in production of output. It is described as follows. First, the underlying production function can be expressed as:

$$y = f(x)e^{-u}, \quad u \geq 0 \tag{2.46}$$

where $y$ is market output produced, $x$ is a vector of inputs used in production, and $u$ is technical inefficiency in production. Technical inefficiency, in this case, is referred to as being output-oriented, i.e., it describes how output can be increased while holding the input mix and quantities constant.

As argued in Kumbhakar and Lovell (2000), only efficiently producing firms survive in the long run, as profit approaches zero in a competitive environment. Allowing for variable profit, it is, therefore, appropriate to apply a short-run framework in which at least one input is modeled as quasi-fixed. Then, the dual variable profit function associated with equation (2.46), conditional on $u$, may be written as:[8]

$$\pi(p,w,q,u) = \pi(pe^{-u},w,q) \tag{2.47}$$

where $p$ is the output price, $w = (w_1,...,w_N)$ and $q = (q_1,...,q_M)$ are vectors of exogenously given input prices and the quasi-fixed inputs, respectively. Hereafter, we refer to $\pi(pe^{-u},w,q)$ as the actual, or observed, variable profit function. As $e^{-u}$ introduces technical inefficiency into the model, the expression in equation (2.47) may be rewritten as:

$$\pi(pe^{-u},w,q) = \pi(p,w,q) \cdot h(p,w,q,u) \tag{2.48}$$

where $\pi(p,w,q)$ is the maximized variable profit function, and $h(p,w,q,u)$ is profit efficiency. By assuming that the underlying production function, $f(x)$, is homogenous of degree $r$ in $x$, profit efficiency is not dependent on exogenously given prices and quasi-fixed inputs, $(p,w,q)$, but only on output-oriented technical efficiency in production, $u$. Thus, rearranging equation (2.48), profit efficiency is defined as:

$$h(u) = \frac{\pi(pe^{-u},w,q)}{\pi(p,w,q)} \leq 1 \tag{2.49}$$

where the maximized variable profit function describes the profit frontier. Hence, profit inefficiency indicates that there is profit loss attributed to output technical inefficiency, and it is interpreted in terms of percentage loss. Only in the case where $u = 0$ does profit efficiency then equal one.

The stochastic profit frontier model may be expressed as:

$$\ln(\pi^{kt}(pe^{-u},w,q)) = \ln(\pi^{kt}(p,w,q;\alpha)) + v^{kt} - u^{kt} \tag{2.50}$$

where $\pi^{kt}(pe^{-u},w,q)$ is the observed profit of firm $k$ in year $t$, and $\pi^{kt}(p,w,q)$ represents the deterministic part of the profit frontier. The error term is divided into two components $v^{kt}$ and $u^{kt}$. Introducing the stochastic part of the frontier, the component $v^{kt}$ arises from random shocks and measurement errors, and these influences are *iid* $N(0,\sigma_v^2)$ and independent of $u^{kt}$, which is a nonnegative random variable that captures technical inefficiency, and is independently (not identically) distributed such that it is obtained by truncation at zero of $N(z^{kt}\delta,\sigma_u^2)$. If the OLS residuals of the expression in Equation (2.50) are negatively skewed, $m_3 < 0$, it indicates technical inefficiency, i.e., $u^{kt} > 0$ (Kumbhakar and Lovell, 2000). Finally, $\sigma_v^2$ and $\sigma_u^2$ are replaced with $\sigma^2 = \sigma_v^2 + \sigma_u^2$ and $\gamma = \sigma_u^2 / (\sigma_v^2 + \sigma_u^2)$.[9]

Technical inefficiency in equation (2.50) is defined as:

$$u^{kt} = z^{kt}\delta + \upsilon^{kt} \tag{2.51}$$

Here $z^{kt} = [z_1^{kt},...,z_J^{kt}]$ is a vector of variables that potentially have an effect on efficiency, and $\delta$ is a vector of parameters to be estimated. The random variable, $\upsilon^{kt} \sim N(0,\sigma_\upsilon^2)$, is truncated by the variable truncation point $-z^{kt}\delta = \upsilon^{kt} - u^{kt}$.

Profit technical inefficiency is then defined as:

$$-u^{\pi,kt} = -\rho \cdot u^{kt} \tag{2.52}$$

where $\rho = 1/(1-r)$, and $u^{\pi,kt}$ is to be interpreted as firm $k$'s percentage profit loss in period $t$ caused by producing output technically inefficient (Kumbhakar, 2001, p. 5). Equation (2.52) shows that profit technical inefficiency is a constant multiple of technical inefficiency, and the profit frontier, $\pi(p,w,q)$, is a neutral transformation of the observed profit function, $\pi(pe^{-u},w,q)$, which means that shifts of the profit function is independent of prices (Kumbhakar, 2001) (compare equation (2.49)). This follows from the underlying technology being homogenous.

Finally, profit technical efficiency is expressed as:

$$PE^{kt} = \exp(-u^{\pi,kt}) = \exp(-\rho u^{kt}) = \exp(-\rho(z^{kt}\delta - \upsilon^{kt})) \tag{2.53}$$

which shows that the smaller the nonnegative profit inefficiency variable, $u^{\pi,kt}$, the more profit efficient is firm $k$ at time $t$. Hence, when $u^{\pi,kt} = 0$, then $PE^{kt} = 1$ and the firm is operating efficiently on the technology frontier.

## 2.6   Notes

1  See Färe and Primont (1995) for a more detailed discussion.
2  Here we have required that $b = 0$, i.e., $b_j = 0$, $j = 1,...,J$. This may be weakened to allow for some $b_j = 0$ implies that $y = 0$.
3  This means that it is not costly to dispose of or waste good output.

4 For additional discussion of this, see Färe and Primont (1995).
5 This is true under CRS and nonincreasing returns to scale.
6 The Shephard's output distance function, which expands both good and bad outputs, would yield values of one for both A and B. The directional distance function, which seeks to increase good output and decrease bad, would also signal efficiency as long as the direction vector was "steeper" than segment AB. Another alternative is to employ a Russell measure, see Färe and Lovell (1978).
7 For a discussion of the existence of a maximum, see Färe and Primont (1995).
8 Following Kumbhakar and Lovell (2000), we assume profit maximization and use duality theory to establish equivalence between the production function in Equation (2.46) and the profit function (see, e.g., Färe and Primont, 1995).
9 To test whether there is any technical inefficiency at all, a significance test of the $\gamma$ estimate can be run (see Coelli, 1996, p. 6).

## 2.7 References

Baumgärtner, S., H. Dykhoff, M. Faber, J. Proops, J. Shiller, 2001. The Concept of Joint Production and Ecological Economics. *Ecological Economics* 36: 365–372.

Chambers, R.G., 1996. A New Look at the Exact Input, Output Productivity and Technical Change Measurement, Maryland Agricultural Experimental Station.

Chambers, R.G., R. Färe, S. Grosskopf, 1996. Productivity Growth in APEC Countries, Pacific. *Economic Review* 1(3): 181–190.

Charnes, A., W.W. Cooper, E. Rhodes, 1978. Measuring the Efficiency of Decision Making Units. *European Journal of Operational Research* 2: 429–444.

Coelli, T.J., 1996. A Guide to FRONTIER Version 4.1: A Computer Program for Frontier Production Function Estimation, CEPA Working Paper No 7/96, Department of Econometrics, University of New England, Armidale, Australia.

Färe, R., S. Grosskopf, F. Hernandez-Sancho, 1999. Environmental Performance: An Index Number Approach, Department of Economics Working Paper, Oregon State University, Corvallis.

Färe, R., S. Grosskopf, C. Pasurka, 2013. Joint Production of Good and Bad Outputs with a Network Application. *Encyclopedia of Energy, Natural Resource, and Environmental Economics* 2: 109–118.

Färe, R., S. Grosskopf, C. Pasurka, 2014. Potential Gains from Trading Bad Outputs: The Case of U.S. Electric Power Plants. *Resource and Energy Economics* 36: 99–112.

Färe, R., C.A. Knox Lovell, 1978. Measuring the Technical Efficiency of Production. *Journal of Economic Theory* 19(1): 150–162.

Färe, R., D. Primont, 1995. *Multi-Output Production and Duality: Theory and Applications*. Kluwer Academic Publishers, Boston.

Førsund, F.R., 2009. Good Modelling of Bad Outputs: Pollution and Multiple-Output Production. *International Review of Environmental and Resource Economics* 3(1): 1–38.

Kemeny, J.G., O. Morgenstern, G.L. Thompson, 1956. A Generalization of the von Neumann Model of an Expanding Economy. *Econometrica* 24: 115–135.

Kumbhakar, S.C., 2001. Estimation of Profit Functions when Profit Is Not Maximum. *American Journal of Agricultural Economics* 83(1): 1–19.

Kumbhakar, S.C., C.A.K. Lovell, 2000. *Stochastic Frontier Analysis*. Cambridge University Press, Cambridge.

Malmquist, S., 1953. Index Numbers and Indifference Curves. *Trabajos de Estadistica* 4(1): 209–242.

Murty, S., R. Robert Russell, S.B. Levkoff, 2012. On Modeling Pollution-Generating Technologies. *Journal of Environmental Economics and Management* 64(1): 117–135.

Shephard, R.W., 1953. *Cost and Production Functions*. Princeton University Press, Princeton, NJ.

Shephard, R.W., 1970. *Theory of Cost and Production Functions*. Princeton University Press, Princeton, NJ.

Shephard, R.W., R. Färe, 1974. The Law of Diminishing Returns. *Zeitschrift für Nationalökonomie* 34: 69–90.

von Neumann, J., 1945–1946. A Model of General Economic Equilibrium. *Review of Economic Studies* 13(33): 1–9.

# 3 Productivity

## Should we include bads?

### 3.1 Introduction

Concerns about whether continual economic growth is consistent with a sustainable society are increasing. In this context, three pillars of society have been identified politically: economic, environmental, and social sustainability. In this chapter, we highlight the issue of measuring economic growth, or productivity growth, given that the society values emission reductions and therefore pursues environmental policy.

Internationally, there is a political consensus on the need for, e.g., common energy and climate policy objectives. A specific example is the EU 2020 strategy, which expresses the necessity of considerably reducing greenhouse gases and making energy consumption more efficient (European Commission, 2010). Hence, it is important to investigate whether air emissions need to be included in productivity measurement, where good outputs and emission reductions both are credited.

The specific purpose of this chapter is to investigate to what extent productivity measurement may be erroneous if not including emissions, treated as by-products in production, i.e., as bad outputs simultaneously produced with good outputs.[1] Based on firm-level data from Swedish manufacturing covering the period 1990 to 2008, we compare two approaches of estimating total factor productivity (TFP) scores, one including bad outputs and the other excluding these outputs. If the resulting productivity scores differ between these approaches, it indicates that excluding bad outputs in productivity measurement leads to erroneous growth accounting.

As we want to account for both good outputs and bad outputs, it is appropriate to base estimations of TFP on a directional output distance function approach, which allows for modeling joint production of good and bad outputs, crediting firms for increasing good outputs and reducing bad outputs.[2]

Considering both environmental and economic firm performance, Chung et al. (1997) developed and applied the Malmquist-Luenberger (ML) productivity index composed of ratios of directional output distance functions. Other studies putting the ML index into practice are, e.g., Jeon and Sickles (2004), Yöruk and Zaim (2005), Kumar (2006), and Yu et al. (2008). Färe et al. (2001) and Weber and Domazlicky (2001) compare two different ML productivity indexes, including and excluding bad outputs. They find that excluding bad outputs from the computations results in an underestimate of TFP growth. Therefore, ignoring emissions from firms' production may bias productivity growth downwards.[3] By contrast, we apply the output-oriented Luenberger productivity indicator introduced by Chambers (1996). The reason is that it allows us to easily aggregate firm-level productivity scores to sector-level scores.

The Luenberger productivity indicator measure is constructed in terms of differences between directional output distance functions rather than ratios. To our knowledge, this particular difference approach has never been applied to address the question of whether excluding bad outputs biases productivity growth accounting. Also, following Chambers et al. (1996), we additively decompose the Luenberger indicator into technical change and efficiency change. The Luenberger indicator and its components can be added over firms, aggregating firm indicators up to an industry indicator. To facilitate aggregation we choose, for all observations, a common direction of expanding and contracting good and bad outputs, respectively. To calculate productivity growth and its components we apply the activity analysis, or the data envelopment analysis (DEA) approach.

The main contribution of the study in this chapter is empirical. This is the first productivity analysis that covers the entire Swedish manufacturing sector, and it includes bad outputs in productivity measurement as well. As already established in earlier literature, it is crucial to include bad outputs, and our analysis provides empirical evidence on how seriously productivity measurement may be biased if bad outputs are not included.

## 3.2   The directional output distance function and Luenberger productivity indicator

To model production technology with jointly produced good and bad outputs, the directional output distance function is employed. Serving as a measure of technical inefficiency, this function gives the maximum expansion of good outputs and contraction of bad outputs, given inputs.

Denote inputs by $x \in \Re_+^N$, good outputs by $y \in \Re_+^M$, and bad (undesirable) outputs by $b \in \Re_+^J$. The production technology is here represented by its output sets

$$P(x) = \{(y,b) : x \text{ can produce } (y,b)\}, x \in \Re_+^N, \tag{3.1}$$

which are assumed closed and bounded (compact) with inputs being strongly disposable, i.e.,

$$x' \geq x \Rightarrow P(x') \geq P(x).$$

In addition, we assume that good and bad outputs are null-joint, i.e.,[4]

$$\text{if } (y,b) \in P(x) \text{ and } b = 0 \text{ then } y = 0,$$

which tells us that good outputs cannot be produced without producing bad outputs, i.e., no fire without smoke. In order to model the idea of abatement diverting resources from production of good outputs, we also assume that good and bad outputs are together weakly disposable, i.e.,[5]

$$\text{if } (y,b) \in P(x) \text{ and } 0 \leq \theta \leq 1 \text{ then } (\theta y, \theta b) \in P(x).$$

Additionally, we assume that good outputs are strongly disposable, i.e.,

$$\text{if } (y,b) \in P(x) \text{ and } y' \leq y \text{ then } (y',b) \in P(x),$$

which says that a good output can be reduced freely without reducing any other good output.

### 3.2.1 The Luenberger productivity indicator including bad output

Letting $g = (g_y, -g_b)$ be a directional vector describing how a $(y,b)$ vector is projected onto the frontier of the output set, the directional output distance function is defined on $P(x)$ as[6]

$$\vec{D}_o(x, y, b; g_y, -g_b) = \max\{\beta : (y + \beta \cdot g_y, b - \beta \cdot g_b) \in P(x)\}. \quad (3.2)$$

The directional output distance function simultaneously expands good outputs and contracts bad outputs. For efficient output vectors on the boundary of $P(x)$, the function takes the value of zero, and for inefficient vectors, positive values. The more inefficient the output vector is, the higher the value of the distance function.

The Luenberger productivity indicator, introduced by Chambers (1996), consists of differences between directional distance functions and compares firm performance in adjacent periods $t$ and $t+1$, i.e.,[7]

$$L_t^{t+1} = \frac{1}{2}\Big[\vec{D}_o^{t+1}(x^t, y^t, b^t; g_y, -g_b) - \vec{D}_o^{t+1}(x^{t+1}, y^{t+1}, b^{t+1}; g_y, -g_b) \\ + \vec{D}_o^t(x^t, y^t, b^t; g_y, -g_b) - \vec{D}_o^t(x^{t+1}, y^{t+1}, b^{t+1}; g_y, -g_b)\Big]. \quad (3.3)$$

$\vec{D}_O^{t+1}$ means that the reference technology is constructed from period $t+1$ data, and the input and output observations $(x^\tau, y^\tau, b^\tau)$, $\tau = t, t+1$ are then compared to that technology. The same holds for the reference technology $\vec{D}_O^t$. No productivity change between $t$ and $t+1$ is indicated by $L_t^{t+1} = 0$, productivity regress by $L_t^{t+1} < 0$, and productivity growth by $L_t^{t+1} > 0$.

Following Chambers et al. (1996), $L_t^{t+1}$ can be decomposed additively into an efficiency component, $LECH_t^{t+1}$, and a technical change component, $LTCH_t^{t+1}$, where

$$LECH_t^{t+1} = \vec{D}_O^t\left(x^t, y^t, b^t; g_y, -g_b\right) - \vec{D}_O^{t+1}\left(x^{t+1}, y^{t+1}, b^{t+1}; g_y, -g_b\right), \quad (3.4)$$

and

$$\begin{aligned}
LTCH_t^{t+1} = \frac{1}{2}\Big[ &\vec{D}_O^{t+1}\left(x^{t+1}, y^{t+1}, b^{t+1}; g_y, -g_b\right) \\
&- \vec{D}_O^t\left(x^{t+1}, y^{t+1}, b^{t+1}; g_y, -g_b\right) \\
&+ \vec{D}_O^{t+1}\left(x^t, y^t, b^t; g_y, -g_b\right) - \vec{D}_O^t\left(x^t, y^t, b^t; g_y, -g_b\right)\Big].
\end{aligned} \quad (3.5)$$

$LECH_t^{t+1}$ measures the change in distance to the frontier of $P(x)$ between periods; $LTCH_t^{t+1}$ measures the shift in the production possibilities frontier. If there is no change in efficiency or the technology, the components in (3.4) and (3.5) take the value of zero. Depending on negative or positive development, these components take values less than zero and values larger than zero, respectively.

In the above model (3.1)–(3.5), the production of bad outputs has been taken into account explicitly. Based on this model, we calculate two different productivity indicators. First, assuming the directional vector $g = (g_y = 1, -g_b = -1)$, a productivity indicator is calculated, where the distance function simultaneously expands good outputs and contracts bad outputs. The other indicator is calculated assuming the directional vector $g = (g_y = 1, -g_b = 0)$, which means that only good outputs are expanded, while bad outputs are held constant.

### 3.2.2   The Luenberger productivity indicator excluding bad output

Excluding bad outputs, the directional output distance function is defined on the output possibilities set

$$\hat{P}(x) = \{y : x \text{ can produce } y\} \quad (3.6)$$

as

$$\vec{D}_O(x, y; g_y) = \max\left\{\beta : (y + \beta \cdot g_y) \in \hat{P}(x)\right\}. \quad (3.7)$$

In this case, the Luenberger productivity indicator is defined as

$$\hat{L}_t^{t+1} = \frac{1}{2}\Big[ \vec{D}_O^{t+1}\big(x^t, y^t; g_y\big) - \vec{D}_O^{t+1}\big(x^{t+1}, y^{t+1}; g_y\big)$$
$$+ \vec{D}_O^t\big(x^t, y^t; g_y\big) - \vec{D}_O^t\big(x^{t+1}, y^{t+1}; g_y\big)\Big], \tag{3.8}$$

with the decomposition

$$\hat{L}_t^{t+1} = \hat{LECH}_t^{t+1} + \hat{LTCH}_t^{t+1}. \tag{3.9}$$

Hence, the model described by (3.6)–(3.9) is similar to the model described by (3.1)–(3.5), with the exception of excluding bad outputs. In this particular case, the directional vector is $g = (g_y = 1)$.

## 3.3 The DEA formulations

To estimate our three Luenberger productivity indicators and compare them and their components, we use nonparametric linear programming techniques. Specifically, we use DEA or activity analysis models. For each productivity indicator, four maximization problems need to be solved; two for within-period distance functions and two for mixed-period distance functions.

### 3.3.1 Model I: including bad outputs with good output expanded and bad output contracted

Assuming the directional vector $g = (g_y, -g_b) = (1, -1)$, credit is given to simultaneous expansion of good outputs and contraction of bad outputs in productivity measurement.[8] In this case, the maximization problem for the mixed-period distance function, $\vec{D}_O^{t+1}(t)$, for observation $(x^{k'}, y^{k'}, b^{k'})$, $k' = 1, ..., K$, is

$$\vec{D}_O^{t+1}\big(x^{k't}, y^{k't}, b^{k't}; 1, -1\big) = \max \beta$$

$$s.t. \qquad \sum_{k=1}^{K} z_k^{t+1} y_{km}^{t+1} \geq y_{k'm}^t + \beta \cdot 1, \, m = 1, ..., M,$$

$$\sum_{k=1}^{K} z_k^{t+1} b_{kj}^{t+1} = b_{k'j}^t - \beta \cdot 1, \, j = 1, ..., J, \tag{3.10}$$

$$\sum_{k=1}^{K} z_k^{t+1} x_{kn}^{t+1} \leq x_{k'n}^t, \, n = 1, ..., N,$$

$$z_k^{t+1} \geq 0, \, k = 1, ..., K.$$

Weak disposability is imposed by the good output inequalities and the bad output equalities.[9] Constant returns to scale holds since the intensity variables, $z_k, k = 1, ..., K$, are just required to be nonnegative. Null-jointness holds when,

$$\sum_{j=1}^{J} b_{kj} > 0, k = 1, ..., K, \text{ and } \sum_{k=1}^{K} b_{kj} > 0, j = 1, ..., J,$$

and our data show this. Similarly, maximization problems for $D_O^{t+1}(t+1)$, $D_O^t(t+1)$ and $D_O^t(t)$ are solved.

### 3.3.2   Model II: including bad outputs with only good output expanded

Assuming the directional vector $g = (g_y, -g_b) = (1, 0)$, Model II is calculated like in (3.10), with the difference that the bad output restrictions become

$$\sum_{k=1}^{K} z_k^{t+1} b_{kj}^{t+1} = b_{k'j}^t, j = 1, ..., J.$$

The only difference compared to Model I is that bad outputs now are not scaled by $\beta$ and, therefore, credit is only given to expansion of good outputs. In other words, it is assumed that technically efficient levels of bad outputs are already produced. In the model, however, bad outputs are still assumed weakly disposable together with good outputs.

### 3.3.3   Model III: excluding bad outputs

By fully excluding bad outputs from the production technology, the maximization problem for the mixed-period distance function, $\vec{D}_O^{t+1}(t)$, is

$$\vec{D}_O^{t+1}\left(x^{k't}, y^{k't}; 1\right) = \max \beta$$

$$\text{s.t.} \quad \sum_{k=1}^{K} z_k^{t+1} y_{km}^{t+1} \geq y_{k'm}^t + \beta \cdot 1, m = 1, ..., M,$$

$$\sum_{k=1}^{K} z_k^{t+1} x_{kn}^{t+1} \leq x_{k'n}^t, n = 1, ..., N,$$

$$z_k^{t+1} \geq 0, k = 1, ..., K.$$

(3.11)

Note that by excluding bad outputs from the production technology, bads are implicitly assumed to be freely disposable (Färe et al., 2001), which is the main difference compared to Model II, where bads are assumed weakly disposable together with good outputs.

In general, the $g$ vector has units of measurement. To avoid this, we follow Shephard (1970, p. 124) and normalize the variables. That is, the variables in estimations are $x_{kn}^t / \bar{x}_n$, $n = 1,...,N$, $y_{km}^t / \bar{y}_m$, $m = 1,...,M$, and $b_{kj}^t / \bar{b}_j$, $j = 1,...,J$, where the "bar" denotes the mean of the variable. Units of measurement are particularly a problem in Model I with the directional vector, $g = (g_y, g_b) = (1, -1)$, scaling both good and bad outputs. To be consistent, and for the purpose of comparing the outcomes of the different models, we also make the normalization when estimating Models II and III.[10]

## 3.4 Data

We use firm-level data on Swedish manufacturing including firms from 12 different sectors, covering the period 1990 to 2008. The data are uniquely detailed and extensive, containing firm-level data on outputs and inputs in production, together with emissions of various air pollutants. All data comes from a unique data selection especially compiled by Statistics Sweden.

The technology modeled in this study consists of one good output index[11] – derived from sales value (kSEK) in 1990 SEK – and three bad outputs (ton), carbon dioxide ($CO_2$), sulfur dioxide ($SO_2$), and nitrogen oxides ($NO_x$). These bad outputs are aggregated into an index (BOI), defined as the weighted mean of $CO_2$, $SO_2$, and $NO_x$.[12] Inputs are capital stock[13] (MSEK), the number of employees, fossil fuels (MWh) and non-fossil fuels (MWh). Tables 3.1 and 3.2 summarize the data over the period studied.

Table 3.2 shows that output has grown by 3.5 percent per year at the industry level, while emissions are practically unchanged. However, there is considerable variation across individual sectors. In Figure 3.1, we plot the emission intensity over time for the whole industry, and it shows a considerable improvement in the period studied. This general pattern is in line with findings in Brännlund et al. (2011), where a similar data set of Swedish manufacturing was studied (1990–2004) but with only one bad output ($CO_2$) included in the performance index.

Table 3.1 Swedish manufacturing data, firm level. Descriptive statistics, mean values 1990–2008 (base = 1990).

| | NOBS | Capital (MSEK) | Worker | Fossil Fuel (MWh) | Non-Fossil Fuel (MWh) | Output (index) | $CO_2$ (ton) | $SO_2$ (ton) | $NO_x$ (ton) |
|---|---|---|---|---|---|---|---|---|---|
| Mining | 476 | 430 (1552) | 278 (742) | 66084 (243002) | 104400 (345164) | 445 (1251) | 20314 (75172) | 25.4 (98.9) | 113 (497.4) |
| Food | 4311 | 101 (298) | 202 (507) | 12255 (56248) | 10029 (28511) | 394 (1032) | 2994 (13909) | 2.1 (13.6) | 2.7 (14.2) |
| Wood | 4499 | 46 (128) | 79 (160) | 1157 (5769) | 18701 (47445) | 154 (343) | 313 (1578) | 1.2 (3.6) | 3.8 (9.7) |
| Pulp/Paper | 1617 | 595 (1158) | 427 (777) | 68154 (131291) | 292817 (660298) | 899 (1669) | 18356 (35715) | 29.1 (63.1) | 39.1 (82.1) |
| Chemical | 1818 | 275 (1231) | 250 (793) | 26119 (100354) | 47132 (147489) | 524 (1932) | 6723 (27388) | 7.5 (45.5) | 6.7 (31.9) |
| Rubber/Plastic | 2069 | 42 (94) | 101 (192) | 2215 (6382) | 5346 (10060) | 115 (230) | 540 (1452) | 0.3 (1.1) | 0.5 (1.8) |
| Stone/Mineral | 1869 | 58 (108) | 142 (216) | 37922 (174896) | 10362 (35729) | 159 (242) | 11346 (56752) | 6.7 (30) | 21.7 (149.9) |
| Iron/Steel | 566 | 211 (507) | 328 (618) | 35418 (115753) | 104864 (318757) | 747 (1573) | 8735 (28664) | 3.6 (13.7) | 8.3 (27.7) |
| Metal | 2972 | 10 (17) | 42 (135) | 581 (2042) | 1421 (4105) | 29 (58) | 148 (509) | 0.1 (0.2) | 0.1 (0.5) |
| Machinery | 6201 | 43 (128) | 166 (404) | 1459 (6160) | 4553 (14401) | 213 (693) | 368 (1364) | 0.2 (0.9) | 0.3 (1.2) |
| Electro | 2211 | 68 (293) | 324 (1399) | 1477 (5195) | 5143 (16379) | 868 (6976) | 393 (1540) | 0.3 (3.6) | 0.3 (1.7) |
| Motor vehicles | 2035 | 385 (1832) | 562 (2097) | 6921 (28908) | 17191 (65268) | 1264 (6316) | 1873 (8256) | 2.4 (16.7) | 1.8 (9) |

Table 3.2 Swedish manufacturing industry data. Mean annual growth rates 1990–2008 (base = 1990).

| | Capital | Workers | Fossil Fuel | Non-Fossil Fuel | Output | $CO_2$ | $SO_2$ | $NO_x$ | BOI |
|---|---|---|---|---|---|---|---|---|---|
| Mining | 0.105 | −0.016 | 0.047 | 0.032 | 0.014 | 0.051 | 0.034 | 0.033 | 0.051 |
| Food | 0.052 | −0.018 | −0.028 | 0.012 | 0.006 | −0.032 | −0.078 | −0.030 | −0.032 |
| Wood | 0.057 | 0.005 | −0.003 | 0.169 | 0.047 | −0.004 | 0.099 | 0.419 | −0.004 |
| Pulp/Paper | 0.039 | −0.028 | 0.024 | 0.042 | 0.013 | 0.022 | 0.016 | 0.049 | 0.022 |
| Chemical | 0.136 | 0.028 | 0.103 | 0.022 | 0.058 | 0.108 | 0.123 | 0.167 | 0.108 |
| Rubber/Plastic | 0.044 | −0.013 | 0.021 | 0.035 | 0.017 | 0.015 | −0.079 | 0.035 | 0.015 |
| Stone/Mineral | 0.036 | −0.016 | −0.005 | 0.010 | 0.012 | −0.005 | −0.017 | −0.008 | −0.005 |
| Iron/Steel | 0.048 | −0.020 | 0.095 | 0.022 | −0.001 | 0.096 | 0.177 | 0.113 | 0.096 |
| Metal | 0.134 | 0.143 | 0.145 | 0.152 | 0.139 | 0.133 | 0.055 | 0.163 | 0.133 |
| Machinery | 0.053 | −0.007 | −0.027 | 0.016 | 0.045 | −0.032 | −0.093 | −0.029 | −0.032 |
| Electro | 0.016 | −0.002 | −0.037 | −0.009 | 0.224 | −0.042 | −0.094 | −0.052 | −0.042 |
| Motor vehicles | 0.078 | −0.005 | −0.031 | 0.016 | 0.069 | −0.029 | −0.024 | −0.025 | −0.029 |
| Industry | 0.055 | −0.015 | 0.001 | 0.036 | 0.035 | 0.0002 | −0.005 | 0.023 | 0.0002 |

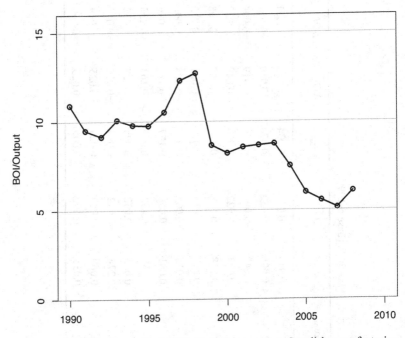

*Figure 3.1* Emission intensity (BOI/output) development, Swedish manufacturing
1990–2008

## 3.5   Results

### 3.5.1   *Average annual productivity growth in sectors and aggregated industry*

The main purpose of this study is to answer the question of whether bad outputs should be included or not when estimating firms' productivity performance. For that purpose, we compare computed productivity change scores generated by three different models, including and excluding bad outputs (BOI). Table 3.3 presents productivity measurements decomposed into efficiency change and technological change for all sectors and for the aggregated industry.

In the case of including bad outputs and crediting both expansion of good outputs and contraction of bad outputs (Model I), all sectors except Mining and Food show a positive development of productivity measured as annual means. For the industry as a whole, development is on average 1.8 percent during 1990–2008 and stems mainly from technological change. The most

Table 3.3 Productivity growth*, efficiency change*, and technical change* of sectors: including and excluding bad outputs (BOI)**

| | Model I including BOI g = (1, −1) | | | Model II including BOI g = (1, 0) | | | Model III excluding BOI g = (1) | | |
|---|---|---|---|---|---|---|---|---|---|
| | PC | EC | TC | PC | EC | TC | PC | EC | TC |
| Mining | −0.014 | 0.015 | −0.029 | 0.004 | 0.166 | −0.163 | 0.011 | 0.010 | 0.001 |
| Food | −0.002 | −0.001 | −0.001 | −0.019 | −0.012 | −0.007 | −0.032 | −0.014 | −0.017 |
| Wood | 0.019 | 0.022 | −0.003 | −0.003 | 0.040 | −0.043 | 0.000 | 0.031 | −0.031 |
| Pulp/Paper | 0.014 | −0.006 | 0.020 | 0.003 | −0.006 | 0.010 | 0.021 | −0.007 | 0.028 |
| Chemical | 0.003 | −0.015 | 0.018 | −0.029 | −0.049 | 0.020 | −0.028 | −0.053 | 0.025 |
| Rubber/Plastic | 0.014 | 0.012 | 0.002 | −0.043 | −0.070 | 0.027 | −0.030 | −0.041 | 0.011 |
| Stone/Mineral | 0.012 | 0.045 | −0.034 | −0.005 | −0.001 | −0.004 | 0.016 | 0.011 | 0.005 |
| Iron/Steel | 0.030 | 0.050 | −0.019 | 0.037 | 0.124 | −0.087 | −0.026 | 0.078 | −0.103 |
| Metal | 0.022 | 0.046 | 0.008 | −0.161 | −0.108 | −0.052 | −0.163 | −0.159 | −0.004 |
| Machinery | 0.023 | −0.003 | 0.026 | 0.027 | −0.094 | 0.121 | 0.033 | −0.101 | 0.133 |
| Electro | 0.050 | −0.155 | 0.205 | 0.061 | −0.086 | 0.147 | 0.065 | −0.097 | 0.162 |
| Motor vehicles | 0.044 | −0.028 | 0.072 | 0.086 | 0.021 | 0.065 | 0.081 | −0.001 | 0.082 |
| Industry | 0.018 | −0.002 | 0.022 | −0.003 | −0.006 | 0.003 | −0.004 | −0.029 | 0.024 |

* Changes are relative to the observed output value; i.e., divide β by observed outputs for each firm.
** PC = productivity change, EC = efficiency change, TC = technical change.

positive development occurs in Electro, on average 5 percent annually. In the case of including bad outputs, but only crediting expansion of good outputs (Model II), productivity change becomes negative for the industry as a whole, averaging −0.3 percent. Sectors showing negative growth rates are now Food, Wood, Chemical, Rubber and Plastic, Stone and Mineral, and Metal. The Vehicles sector now shows the most positive development, 8.6 percent, followed by the Electro sector, 6.1 percent.

Model III, excluding bad outputs entirely, also shows poorer productivity development in comparison with the results shown by Model I. The productivity level for the aggregated industry now becomes nearly unchanged during the period in study, as the development is on average only 0.2 percent. The reason is that the positive technological change is neutralized by a negative efficiency change. At the sector level, results do not show an obvious pattern and quite a few sectors generate negative productivity rates − Food, Chemical, Rubber and Plastic, and Metal. Again, the most positive growth rates occur in the Vehicles and Electro sectors, 8.1 and 6.5 percent, respectively.

Models II and III showing poorer productivity development is in line with findings in Färe et al. (2001) and Weber and Domazlicky (2001). These models, not crediting emission reductions in productivity measurement, are expected to generate poorer productivity change scores if firms in reality have diverted resources from production of good outputs to reduction of emissions.

In Figure 3.2, the industry's accumulated development of productivity and its components are displayed for the period from 1990 to 2008.[14] Here, we visually see the difference between crediting and not crediting reduction of bad outputs in productivity measurement. It is also clear that Models II and III, not crediting reduction of bad outputs, produce quite similar pattern of development, though on different levels. The difference should mainly be due to bad and good outputs being treated as together weakly disposable in Model II, and bad outputs as freely disposable in Model III by being excluded from the production technology.

Also, it is clear that productivity change mainly comes from technology change.

The results presented above visually indicate that different directional vectors, and including and excluding bad outputs, in productivity measurement generate different levels of productivity growth scores. However, whether this is actually the case needs to be tested formally.

### 3.5.2   *Formally testing for differences between models*

To test for differences in computed productivity levels between models, we perform two different tests − Wilcoxon and kernel density tests.

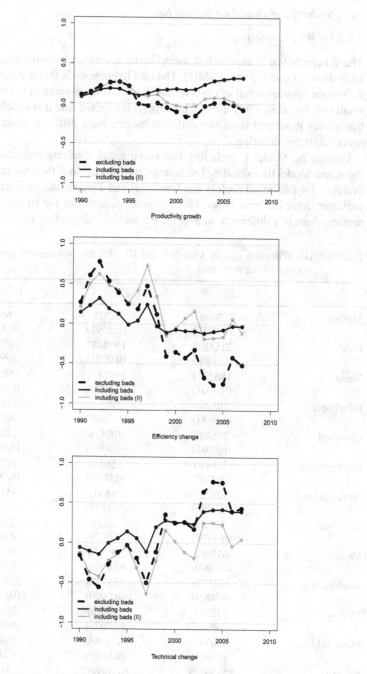

*Figure 3.2* Productivity change, efficiency change, and technical change in Swedish manufacturing during 1990–2008

### 3.5.2.1   *Wilcoxon test*

The Wilcoxon test is used to test for differences between paired scores for each decision-making unit (DMU). The null hypothesis is that the median difference between a pair of observations is zero. If the $p$-value of the test is small (say less than 0.05), the null hypothesis is rejected, and it is concluded that scores generated from two different models have different ranks and accordingly are differing.

Comparing Model I, including bad outputs and crediting reduction of them, and Model III, excluding bad outputs, we can conclude from the results in Table 3.4 that in all sectors but Iron/Steel and Electro, the productivity indicators have different ranks. This outcome suggests that for 10 out of 12 sectors, there is a difference in average productivity depending on whether

*Table 3.4* The Wilcoxon test on Models I and III (H0: the two models generate scores with the same rank)*

|  | *PC* | *EC* | *TC* |
|---|---|---|---|
| Mining | 7696 (0.0217) | 6700 (0.5593) | 6606 (0.5726) |
| Food | 2155888 (0.0000) | 1993477 (0.0001) | 1852955 (0.6654) |
| Wood | 1862874 (0.0001) | 1957171 (0.0000) | 1502800 (0.0000) |
| Pulp/Paper | 205288 (0.0083) | 230360 (0.7608) | 218024 (0.2757) |
| Chemical | 295407 (0.0005) | 300119 (0.0000) | 240944 (0.0234) |
| Rubber/Plastic | 313480 (0.0026) | 326040 (0.0000) | 247838 (0.0003) |
| Stone/Mineral | 329523 (0.0095) | 288403 (0.1891) | 352523 (0.0000) |
| Iron/Steel | 19724 (0.4998) | 15330 (0.0076) | 22694 (0.0033) |
| Metal | 637502 (0.0000) | 559828 (0.0009) | 541884 (0.0259) |
| Machinery | 3925204 (0.0000) | 4550778 (0.0000) | 2309698 (0.0000) |
| Electro | 352751 (0.4046) | 425486 (0.0000) | 255204 (0.0000) |
| Motor vehicles | 420341 (0.0003) | 446966 (0.0000) | 306386 (0.0000) |
| Industry | 85356778 (0.0000) | 87266682 (0.0000) | 68348869 (0.0000) |

* Numbers in parentheses are $p$-values.

bad output is included or not. Referring back to Table 3.3 and Figure 3.2, this suggests that the productivity change score is lower for the aggregated industry on average when excluding bad outputs from the production technology. To conclude, it does matter whether bads are included or not. However, looking at individual sectors, this conclusion is not as obvious.

The results of comparing Model I and II, crediting and not crediting reduction of bad outputs, respectively, are presented in Table 3.5.

Generally, the same conclusions can be made as in the case of comparing Model I and Model III. Recall the difference between Models II and III; in Model II bad outputs are included in the production technology and assumed weakly disposable together with good outputs. However, in Model III bad outputs are fully excluded and, therefore, implicitly assumed

*Table 3.5* The Wilcoxon test on Models I and II (H0: the two models generate scores with the same rank)*

|                 | PC                    | EC                    | TC                    |
|-----------------|-----------------------|-----------------------|-----------------------|
| Mining          | 7686<br>(0.0226)      | 6814<br>(0.4350)      | 6762<br>(0.4899)      |
| Food            | 2127156<br>(0.0000)   | 1947544<br>(0.0047)   | 1921502<br>(0.0343)   |
| Wood            | 1857440<br>(0.0001)   | 1880150<br>(0.0000)   | 1602767<br>(0.0044)   |
| Pulp/Paper      | 218466<br>(0.2745)    | 223795<br>(0.6809)    | 234858<br>(0.4049)    |
| Chemical        | 294530<br>(0.0006)    | 294810<br>(0.0002)    | 244432<br>(0.0577)    |
| Rubber/Plastic  | 322787<br>(0.0001)    | 323911<br>(0.0001)    | 266638<br>(0.0870)    |
| Stone/Mineral   | 332642<br>(0.0032)    | 290725<br>(0.2746)    | 351857<br>(0.0000)    |
| Iron/Steel      | 22292<br>(0.0085)     | 17096<br>(0.1848)     | 22382<br>(0.0069)     |
| Metal           | 597354<br>(0.0000)    | 479171<br>(0.0699)    | 642000<br>(0.0000)    |
| Machinery       | 3883941<br>(0.0000)   | 4320252<br>(0.0000)   | 2630438<br>(0.0000)   |
| Electro         | 360576<br>(0.1183)    | 387484<br>(0.0001)    | 297544<br>(0.0001)    |
| Motor vehicles  | 405544<br>(0.0175)    | 412574<br>(0.0032)    | 336322<br>(0.0016)    |
| Industry        | 84609363<br>(0.0000)  | 83215164<br>(0.0000)  | 73757600<br>(0.0002)  |

* Numbers in parentheses are *p*-values.

freely disposable. Taken together this indicates that, if firms in reality are diverting resources from production of good outputs to reduction of bad outputs, bad outputs should not only be included in productivity measurement, but credit should also be given to reduction of bad outputs. That is, among the three models, Model I should be used or otherwise productivity development is underestimated. This conclusion is further confirmed by the results of comparing Models II and III in Table 3.6.

Giving no credit to reduction of bad outputs, it does not matter for productivity measurement whether bad outputs are included or not in the production technology ($p$-value is 0.5665). Crucial is to include bad outputs together with giving credit to firms that actually reduce bad outputs, as done in Model I.

*Table 3.6* The Wilcoxon test on Models II and III (H0: the two models generate scores with the same rank)*

|  | PC | EC | TC |
| --- | --- | --- | --- |
| Mining | 5488 (0.3197) | 5911 (0.9709) | 5674 (0.5080) |
| Food | 1818127 (0.9803) | 1832395 (0.6681) | 1796394 (0.4673) |
| Wood | 1642874 (0.9453) | 1855500 (0.0000) | 1435550 (0.0000) |
| Pulp/Paper | 203694 (0.0412) | 230762 (0.2476) | 189918 (0.0001) |
| Chemical | 254440 (0.8851) | 252537 (0.8943) | 266860 (0.3912) |
| Rubber/Plastic | 270728 (0.8780) | 280918 (0.1639) | 256264 (0.0317) |
| Stone/Mineral | 224791 (0.0000) | 258840 (0.2645) | 267550 (0.1051) |
| Iron/Steel | 15794 (0.0329) | 16531 (0.0967) | 19790 (0.4043) |
| Metal | 572976 (0.0000) | 573660 (0.0000) | 444186 (0.0001) |
| Machinery | 3347522 (0.2784) | 3717352 (0.0000) | 2939152 (0.0000) |
| Electro | 309364 (0.0276) | 367818 (0.0064) | 302061 (0.0011) |
| Motor vehicles | 393182 (0.0819) | 412452 (0.0009) | 327914 (0.0002) |
| Industry | 73607326 (0.5051) | 78805136 (0.0000) | 67907826 (0.0000) |

* Numbers in parentheses are *p*-values.

### 3.5.2.2   *Kernel density bootstrap test*

As a complement to the Wilcoxon tests, we further compare visually the estimated outcomes of Models I and III, by using kernel density plots. In addition, bootstrap hypothesis tests of equal densities and permutation tests are performed (p-values presented in Kernel plot figures). A permutation test is a type of statistical significance test in which the distribution of the test statistic under the null hypothesis is obtained by calculating all possible values of the test statistic under rearrangements of the labels (the two different models in our case) on the observed data points (see, e.g., Bowman and Azzalini, 1997). In Figure 3.3, the Kernel density plots, along with *P*-values of the bootstrap tests, are presented (see Appendix 3B for individual sectors).

It is visually clear that the densities are quite different, and the bootstrap tests confirm this.[15] Again, in the case of crediting reduction of bad outputs, it seems to matter whether they are included or not.

## 3.6   Conclusions and discussion

The main purpose of this study has been to investigate whether bad outputs should be included or not in productivity measurement among firms. The methodological framework was based on the directional output distance function approach, which allows for modeling joint production of good and bad outputs. To explicitly compute TFP growth and its components, efficiency change and technological change, we applied the Luenberger productivity indicator constructed in terms of differences between directional output distance functions.

Three different models of Luenberger productivity indicators were explicitly computed. Models I and II included bad outputs in the production technology under the assumption of bad and good outputs being together weakly disposable. By this assumption, reduction of bad outputs comes at a cost, as resources are necessarily diverted from production of good outputs. The only difference between Model I and Model II was that the former credited simultaneous expansion of good outputs and reduction of bad outputs, and the latter only expansion of good outputs. In Model III, only crediting expansion of good outputs, bad outputs were fully excluded and, therefore, implicitly assumed being freely disposable. The productivity measurements were performed on firm-level data from Swedish manufacturing covering the period from 1990 to 2008.

Generally, based on the experience of this study, we argue that the choice of model is important when measuring productivity development. For instance, if society values reduced emission of pollutants, pollution abatement activities among firms and sectors and on a national level should be

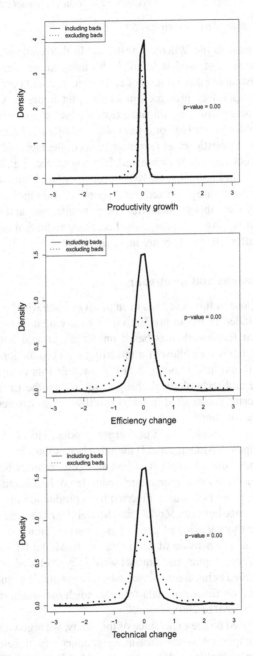

*Figure 3.3* Kernel densities for productivity change scores generated by Models I and III, respectively (H0 = equal distributions) in Swedish manufacturing

accounted for in productivity measurement. However, by excluding bad outputs, these activities are ignored and productivity measurement will underestimate productivity growth from a welfare point of view.[16] To avoid growth accounting errors in this case, bad outputs should not only be included but also reduction of these outputs should be credited. Referring to the directional output distance function approach, this means that a directional vector that credits simultaneous expansion of good outputs and contraction of bad outputs should be chosen. In our study, performing productivity measurement by both including bad outputs and crediting reduction generally resulted in significantly higher productivity growth scores. One possible reason for this outcome would be that firms within Swedish manufacturing actually diverted resources to pollution abatement activities during the period in study.

## 3.7   Notes

1 It is sometimes suggested that emissions could be modeled as input factors in production. However, as shown in, e.g., Färe and Grosskopf (2003) and Førsund (2009), this may be inappropriate.

2 For an introduction to directional distance functions see, e.g., Färe and Grosskopf (2003).

3 This underestimate results from emissions being reduced and the fact that reducing emissions diverts input resources from production of the marketed good output.

4 This assumption can be justified using thermodynamics, see Färe et al. (2013).

5 This assumption is being challenged by Førsund (2009).

6 This is a special case of the shortage function; see Luenberger (1995).

7 See Färe and Grosskopf (2004) for a detailed derivation of the indicator.

8 Commonly, studies assume the directional vector $g = (y, -b)$ (e.g., Chung et al., 1997; Färe et al., 2001; Weber and Domazlicky, 2001). Here, we assume $g = (1, -1)$ to facilitate aggregating firm indicators up to an industry indicator (see, e.g., Färe and Grosskopf, 2004).

9 Note that in the DEA analyses, the property of good and bad outputs being together weakly disposable is implemented as advocated in Färe and Grosskopf (2003). This procedure has been questioned in Kuosmanen (2005) and further discussed in Färe and Grosskopf (2009) and Kuosmanen and Podinovski (2009).

10 Also, normalization improves the estimation results in terms of fewer infeasible solutions.

11 Sales (a price vector multiplied by an output vector at the firm level) are divided by a sector-level producer price index to proxy output.

12 We first tried to handle the three bad outputs separately in the estimations. However, this resulted in too many infeasible solutions.

13 The capital stock is calculated by using gross investment data and the perpetual inventory method. Starting values in 1990 are created assuming that the capital stock is in steady state so that capital equals investment divided by depreciation rate (set to 0.08).

14 In Appendix 3A, we present productivity plots for all individual sectors.

15 Note that, when performing the bootstrap tests, the Iron and Steel sector is divided into two individual subsectors.
16 However, note that if some firms are not reducing emissions, their productivity will be "overstated" if bads are ignored.

## 3.8 References

Bowman, A.W., A. Azzalini, 1997. *Applied Smoothing Techniques for Data Analysis: The Kernel Approach with S-Plus Illustrations*. Oxford University Press, Oxford.

Brännlund, R., T. Lundgren, P-O. Marklund, 2011. Environmental Performance and Climate Policy. Centre for Environmental and Resource Economics, CERE Working Paper 2011: 6, Department of Economics, Umeå University, Umeå, Sweden.

Chambers, R.G., 1996. A New Look at Exact Input, Output, and Productivity Measurement, Department of Agricultural and Resource Economics. WP 96–05 (Revised October 1998), the University of Maryland, College Park.

Chambers, R.G., R. Färe, S. Grosskopf, 1996. Productivity Growth in APEC Countries. *Pacific Economic Review* 1(3): 181–190.

Chung, Y.H., R. Färe, S. Grosskopf, 1997. Productivity and Undesirable Outputs: A Directional Distance Function Approach. *Journal of Environmental Management* 51(3): 229–240.

European Commission, 2010. A Strategy for Smart, Sustainable and Inclusive Growth. Communication from the Commission, COM(2010) 2020 Final.

Färe, R., S. Grosskopf, 2003. Nonparametric Productivity Analysis with Undesirable Outputs: Comment. *American Journal of Agricultural Economics* 85(4): 1070–1074.

Färe, R., S. Grosskopf, 2004. *New Directions: Efficiency and Productivity*. Springer Science & Business Media, Inc., New York.

Färe, R., S. Grosskopf, 2009. A Comment on Weak Disposability in Nonparametric Production Analysis. *American Journal of Agricultural Economics* 91(2): 535–538.

Färe, R., S. Grosskopf, C.A. Pasurka, Jr., 2001. Accounting for Air Pollution Emissions in Measures of State Manufacturing Productivity Growth. *Journal of Regional Science* 41(3): 381–409.

Färe, R., S. Grosskopf, C. Pasurka, 2013. Joint Production of Good and Bad Outputs with a Network Application. *Encyclopedia of Energy, Natural Resource, and Environmental Economics* 2: 109–118.

Førsund, F.R., 2009. Good Modelling of Bad Outputs: Pollution and Multiple-Output Production. *International Review of Environmental and Resource Economics* 3(1): 1–38.

Jeon, B.M., R.C. Sickles, 2004. The Role of Environmental Factors in Growth Accounting. *Journal of Applied Econometrics* 19(5): 567–591.

Kumar, S., 2006. Environmentally Sensitive Productivity Growth: A Global Analysis Using Malmquist-Luenberger Index. *Ecological Economics* 56(2): 280–293.

Kuosmanen, T., 2005. Weak Disposability in Nonparametric Production Analysis with Undesirable Outputs. *American Journal of Agricultural Economics* 87(4): 1077–1082.

Kuosmanen, T., V. Podinovski, 2009. Weak Disposability in Nonparametric Production Analysis: Reply to Färe and Grosskopf. *American Journal of Agricultural Economics* 91(2): 539–545.

Luenberger, D., 1995. *Microeconomic Theory.* McGraw-Hill, Boston.

Shephard, R.W., 1970. *Theory of Cost and Production Functions.* Princeton University Press, Princeton.

Weber, W.L., B. Domazlicky, 2001. Productivity Growth and Pollution in State Manufacturing. *The Review of Economics and Statistics* 83(1): 195–199.

Yöruk, B.K., O. Zaim, 2005. Productivity Growth in OECD Countries: A Comparison with Malmquist Indices. *Journal of Comparative Economics* 33(2): 401–420.

Yu, M.M., S.H. Hsu, C.C. Chang, D.H. Lee, 2008. Productivity Growth of Taiwan's Major Domestic Airports in the Presence of Aircraft Noise. *Transportation Research Part E, Logistics and Transportation Review* 44(3): 543–554.

## 3.9   **Appendix 3A**

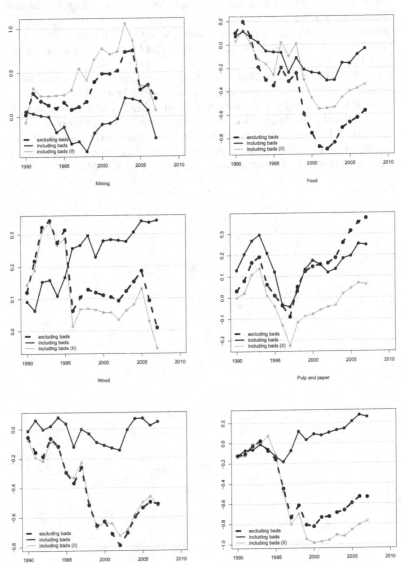

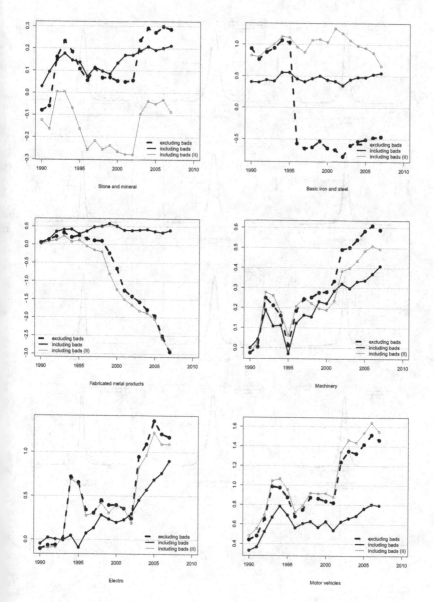

## 3.10 Appendix 3B

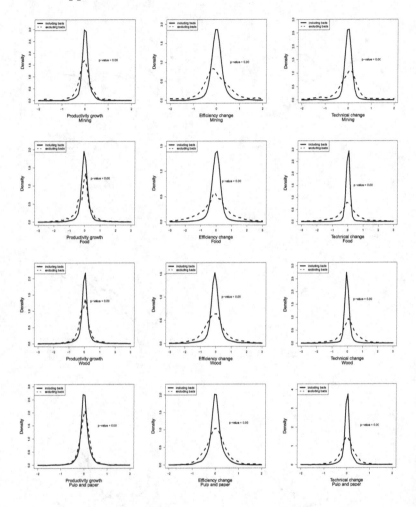

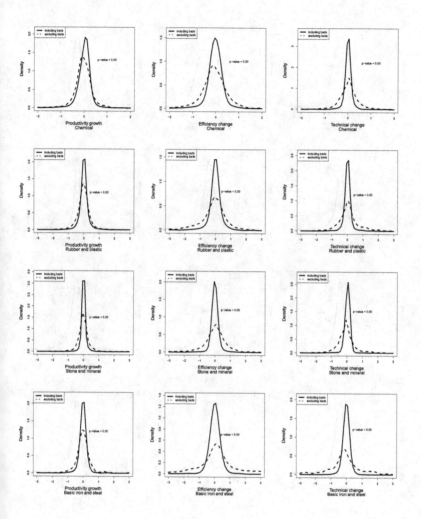

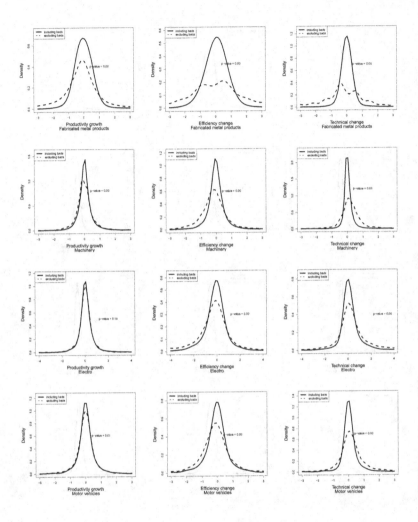

# 4 Environmental performance and productivity

## The role of national and EU-level climate policy

This chapter takes a closer look at how firms' environmental performance and productivity are affected by Swedish national climate policy and the EU ETS. The chapter is a summary of two published studies, Brännlund et al. (2014) and Lundgren et al. (2015). Both studies use performance measurements discussed in Chapter 2: the environmental performance index and the Luenberger productivity indicator (with and without bads). The two studies investigate similar questions but use different methods and time periods. Brännlund et al. (2014) derive an environmental performance index reflecting carbon intensity in production for manufacturing and its sectors and investigate the role of the Swedish $CO_2$ tax during the period 1990–2004. Lundgren et al. (2015) derive a Luenberger productivity indicator and explore how productivity itself, technological development, and technological efficiency in the pulp and paper sector are affected by Swedish and EU climate policies during 1998–2008.

The main results show that (1) the Swedish $CO_2$ tax has significantly affected the environmental performance – in terms of carbon intensity in production – in Swedish manufacturing during 1990–2004 and (2) national- and EU-level carbon prices were most likely too low to incentivize "green" investments that could have increased technological development in the Swedish pulp and paper industry during 1998–2008.

## 4.1 Industrial environmental (carbon) performance and the Swedish $CO_2$ tax, 1990–2004

Brännlund et al. (2014) derive and evaluate a measurement of environmental performance (EP) in Swedish manufacturing during 1990 to 2004 and explore its determinants, especially the Swedish $CO_2$ tax. The analysis is empirical and adopts a micro-economic perspective. Concerning EP, the analysis presented in this chapter is linked to the discussion of decoupling of output production and emissions (see, e.g., Azar et al., 2002), and the

Environmental Kuznets Curve (see, e.g., Grossman and Krueger, 1995; Dinda, 2004). Both of these concepts are connected to breaking the link between growth in emissions and growth in produced output. The firm-level data, combined with data on $CO_2$ tax payments, give a unique opportunity to shed light on pertinent policy issues, here the effectiveness of a $CO_2$ tax.

Studies on aggregated levels provide important information on EP in society. But it is also important to understand EP from a firm-level micro-perspective. Total emissions originate from individual sources with different EP and preconditions of enhancing its performance. We add to the literature by assessing the impact of actual $CO_2$ taxation on EP, which is measured as emission intensity change (not level). Further, our study concerns an industry-wide sample of 13 sectors in manufacturing, which is unseen in previous studies, and our panel data spans a relatively long period.

When assessing the impact of climate policy, it is reasonable to examine how firms respond to the policy, which we achieve by applying an emission intensity change index, an index founded in production theory. A Malmquist-type index is used to evaluate EP at the firm level separately for all sectors in Swedish manufacturing. In the index literature, this kind of indicator is usually referred to as "environmental performance" (see Chapter 2), since it can be expanded to include any number of good and bad outputs. Tyteca (1996) reviews indicators of firm-level environmental performance using linear programming techniques. Zhou et al. (2008) survey data envelopment analyses (DEA) with focus on energy and environmental studies. The study presented here derives and calculates EP according to, e.g., Färe et al. (2006).

### 4.1.1   The environmental performance index

See Chapter 2 or Brännlund et al. (2014) for a complete derivation and discussion of this index. The components of the EP index are quantity indexes that are constructed as ratios of Shephard distance functions. Such an index constitutes a simple measure of EP by calculating how much of the change in the good output(s) is produced per change in the emitted pollutant(s).

An empirical EP index for a single good output (production output; $y$) and a single bad output (carbon dioxide emissions; $b$) for firm $i$ in sector $j$ between time period $t$ and $t + 1$ can be formulated as simply as:

$$EP_{i,j}^{t,t+1} = \frac{y_{i,j}^{k,t+1} / b_{i,j}^{k,t+1}}{y_{i,j}^{k,t} / b_{i,j}^{k,t}} \tag{4.1}$$

In relation to one (1), which means no change, a positive (negative) change in EP means that $CO_2$ intensity or emissions per output unit has increased (decreased). The index is easily aggregated to sector or industry level. The simplicity of this index is due to properties of the distance functions, which means we can calculate it by using only the quantities of the good and bad in two consecutive periods.

### 4.1.2 Empirics

The aim is to assess what factors affected EP in Swedish industrial sectors. The expectation is that firms' EP has been affected principally by the cost of using fossil fuels and the cost of emissions; that is, the price of fossil fuel and the $CO_2$ tax. There is also reason to believe that there is a substantial heterogeneity in how firms' EP is affected. Firms with a large fuel cost share may have less potential to improve their EP due to technological constraints. However, it may also be the case that more fuel intensive firms/sectors are more motivated to cut emissions because there are significant cost savings to be achieved by increasing EP. For this reason, we include the cost share for fossil fuels as an explanatory variable. A variable that reflects capital intensity is included in the empirical specification. One may argue that capital-intensive firms have more difficulties decreasing their environmental impact due to the substantial energy amounts that are associated with a large capital stock. On the other hand, firms with high capital intensity may be more motivated to save energy and invest relatively more in energy saving technologies, and thus improve EP. The effect of fuel and capital intensity on EP is in the end an empirical question. Finally, the size of a firm, technological progress, and an increased overall environmental awareness in society may impact EP. The effect of size is not obvious, but technological progress and environmental awareness/pressure are expected to have a positive impact. Size is measured as size dummy (four classes) derived from number of employees. Technological progress and increased societal environmental awareness/pressure are proxied by a time-trend variable.

The empirical model is specified so that EP is governed by previous period $CO_2$ tax ($\tau$) and price of fossil fuels ($pf$), the cost share of previous period fossil fuels ($sfuel$), capital intensity (capital stock over total employees, $kapin$), a size effect ($size$), and a general time-trend ($trend$), possibly nonlinear. A log-linear specification is chosen:

$$\ln(EP_{i,j}^{t,t+1}) = c_{i,j} + a_{1,j} \ln(\tau_{i,j}^t) + a_{2,j} \ln(pf_{i,j}^t) + a_{3,j} \ln(sfuel_{i,j}^t)$$
$$+ a_{4,j} \ln(kapin_{i,j}^t) + \sum_{size=1}^{4-1} a_{5size,j} size_{i,j}^t + a_{6,j} trend \quad (4.2)$$
$$+ a_{7,j} (trend)^2 + e_{i,j}^{t+1}.$$

If the parameter associated with the tax, $a_{1,j}$, is larger than the fossil fuel price parameter, $a_{2,j}$, there is indication of a "signaling" effect; i.e., aside from the pure price effect of a tax change, the firms also respond to the signal that the tax sends. Equation (4.2) is estimated with panel data methods, with both fixed effects (FE) and random effects (RE). The significance of the FE model is validated with an $F$-test to check whether a model with individual intercepts is significantly different from a model with a common intercept. A Hausman test is performed to check the difference between FE and RE estimates. Only the most relevant model estimates are commented on.

### 4.1.3   Data: a balanced panel data set 1990–2004 for Swedish industry

The data set used in this study is a firm-level balanced panel covering the years 1990 to 2004 for Swedish manufacturing sectors. This period of study is relevant for several reasons. The $CO_2$ tax was introduced in 1991 and the EU emission trading system (ETS) started in 2005. After 2005, the $CO_2$ tax was gradually phased out for ETS firms. This means the period analyzed includes the critical years for the tax, and problems with the ETS "disturbing" the estimates are avoided.

Table 4.1 presents the industry sector classification as well as some relevant descriptive statistics of the sample we use in the empirical analysis.

From the table above, it is clear that the $CO_2$ tax rate varies across and within sectors; the sector tax rate ranges from 0.04 to 0.15 SEK/kg. The price of fossil fuels also varies across and within sectors, but less than the tax does. The variation is due to different fuel mixes across and within sectors. The cost shares for fossil fuel are small, ranging from 1 percent in the Electro, Machinery, and Printing industries to the most fuel-intensive sectors Stone/Mineral and Mining, with a 10 percent cost share. The most capital-intensive sector is Mining, while the other sectors do not deviate much compared to the average for Manufacturing.

Figure 4.1 displays the median and variation of the $CO_2$ tax for all firms for each year. The height of the box is the difference between the 75th and 25th percentiles, and the horizontal line within each box represents the median. The $CO_2$ tax ranges from zero to approximately 0.20 SEK/kg. The variation within sectors is more pronounced than across sectors (looking at the median).

### 4.1.4   Results: environmental performance and effects of the CO₂ tax, 1990–2004

First, results for the EP index are presented on the sector level as averaged values 1990–2004. Second, we have a look at the impacts of, *inter alia*, the effects on EP of the $CO_2$ tax.

*Table 4.1* Descriptive statistics, mean values, sector level, 1990–2004 (standard deviation in parenthesis). Base year 1990

| Description | NOBS | Output (index) | $CO_2$ Tons | $CO_2$ tax SEK/kilo | Price fuel SEK/kWh | Cost share fuel | Capital intensity TSEK |
|---|---|---|---|---|---|---|---|
| Manufacturing | 21030 | 296502 (745327) | 8457 (61011) | 0.11 (0.08) | 0.35 (0.18) | 0.03 (0.05) | 1436 (2597) |
| Mining | 193 | 373993 (681809) | 23893 (59174) | 0.08 (0.07) | 0.28 (0.12) | 0.10 (0.08) | 2733 (2524) |
| Food | 2056 | 343003 (362173) | 3672 (8531) | 0.15 (0.06) | 0.29 (0.45) | 0.05 (0.05) | 1375 (2558) |
| Textile | 403 | 119323 (116808) | 1737 (3403) | 0.13 (0.08) | 0.34 (0.18) | 0.03 (0.05) | 1079 (1385) |
| Wood | 1820 | 191341 (177345) | 2312 (11631) | 0.04 (0.06) | 0.36 (0.18) | 0.03 (0.03) | 1704 (2162) |
| Pulp/Paper | 1292 | 609754 (731287) | 35351 (101467) | 0.13 (0.07) | 0.24 (0.15) | 0.04 (0.05) | 1566 (1573) |
| Printing | 959 | 84040 (117530) | 253 (798) | 0.06 (0.08) | 0.49 (0.21) | 0.01 (0.01) | 1739 (3144) |
| Chemical | 1021 | 507796 (1225336) | 37242 (149990) | 0.12 (0.08) | 0.28 (0.19) | 0.04 (0.06) | 1840 (2929) |
| Rubber/Plastic | 947 | 133501 (165630) | 916 (2438) | 0.12 (0.08) | 0.37 (0.18) | 0.03 (0.05) | 1120 (1410) |
| Stone/Mineral | 1060 | 110269 (119365) | 33154 (168245) | 0.14 (0.07) | 0.24 (0.13) | 0.10 (0.13) | 1375 (1688) |
| Iron/Steel | 2831 | 278699 (696952) | 6709 (29958) | 0.14 (0.07) | 0.35 (0.17) | 0.03 (0.05) | 1593 (5192) |
| Machinery | 2677 | 209396 (340045) | 711 (7187) | 0.11 (0.08) | 0.39 (0.17) | 0.01 (0.02) | 1213 (2599) |
| Electro | 1095 | 391016 (1000759) | 390 (754) | 0.11 (0.08) | 0.41 (0.19) | 0.01 (0.01) | 1183 (3631) |
| Motor vehicles | 1131 | 676418 (1941923) | 2426 (8977) | 0.14 (0.07) | 0.34 (0.15) | 0.02 (0.03) | 957 (1340) |

Source: Brännlund et al., 2014

Sector and industry level indexes are presented in Figure 4.2. The change in $CO_2$ and production, $\Delta CO2 = CO_{2,t+1}/ CO_{2,t}$, and $\Delta Y = Y_{t+1}/ Y_t$, are also presented to show the components and decomposition of EP. Tables with year-by-year sector-level indexes are described in an appendix in Brännlund et al. (2014). Note that in the subsequent empirical analysis, firm-level indexes are used.

Figure 4.2 shows that all subsectors, energy and non-energy-intensive firms, and manufacturing as a whole, have improved EP between 1991 and 2004, i.e., EP > 1. Electro, Chemical, and Motor vehicles display the best performance with average annual growth rates ranging from 7 percent

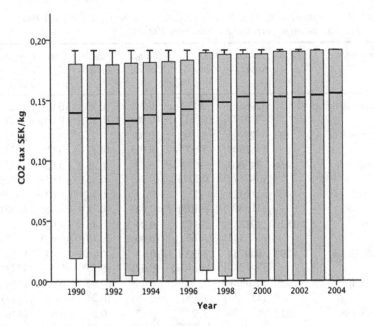

*Figure 4.1* The effective $CO_2$ tax, SEK/kg

Source: Brännlund et al., 2014

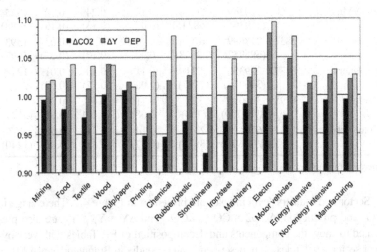

*Figure 4.2* Environmental performance in Swedish industry 1991 to 2004; mean values, sector by sector, and manufacturing as a whole, decomposed into changes in emissions and changes in production

Source: Brännlund et al., 2014

to 10 percent, while the EP in Pulp/Paper improved only marginally. EP's components, $\Delta CO2$ and $\Delta Y$, indicate that almost all sectors experienced falling emissions while production is increasing: $\Delta CO2 < 0$ and $\Delta Y > 0$. Exceptions are Pulp/Paper and Wood, where emissions have increased moderately, but still at slower rate than production. A likely explanation for the increase in emissions is that the forest industry, especially Pulp/Paper, in the 1970s and 1980s made substantial energy efficiency investments, and therefore the increase in $CO_2$ emissions since 1990 is mainly due to increased production.

Figure 4.3 shows the (cumulative) development of EP and its components for manufacturing (all sectors).

Manufacturing as a whole has improved its EP by about 45 percent, which is made possible by decreasing emissions by almost 10 percent while at the same time increasing production by around 35 percent (see Figure 4.3). Together with the sector level results, this shows that there has been a decoupling between production and emissions in Swedish manufacturing. Next is the analysis of the determinants of EP.

In Table 4.2, the results from estimating Equation (4.2) is presented (for selected parameters and diagnostics).

Table 4.2 shows that EP for overall manufacturing is sensitive but inelastic to both the tax and the fuel price; elasticities are 0.313 and 0.137,

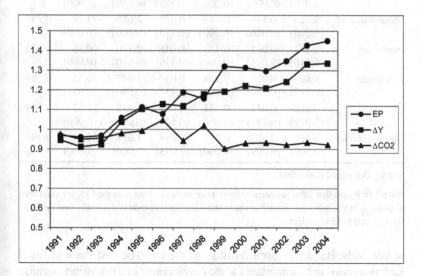

*Figure 4.3* Cumulative environmental performance, Swedish manufacturing
Source: Brännlund et al., 2014

*Table 4.2* Determinants of firm-level environmental performance (EP). Results for selected parameters and diagnostics from estimating Equation (4.2). *P*-values in parenthesis

| Estimates and diagnostics → Sectors ↓ | $CO_2$ tax | Fuel price | Fuel share | Capital intensity | F-test FE vs OLS | Hausman test RE vs FE* | Adj. $R^2$ |
|---|---|---|---|---|---|---|---|
| Manufacturing | 0.313[□] (0.000) | 0.137 (0.000) | 0.571 (0.000) | −0.043 (0.143) | 2.452 (0.000) | 143.9 (0.000) | 0.242 |
| Mining | 0.100 (0.282) | −0.041 (0.697) | 0.762 (0.000) | 0.520 (0.066) | 2.756 (0.033) | 34.24 (0.000) | 0.354 |
| Food | 0.107 (0.003) | 0.056 (0.042) | 0.216 (0.000) | −0.001 (0.959) | 2.087 (0.000) | 31.99 (0.000) | 0.208 |
| Textile | 0.580[□] (0.001) | 0.195 (0.000) | 0.087 (0.009) | 0.056 (0.311) | 1.417 (0.110) | 7.747 (0.101) | 0.079 |
| Wood | 0.346 (0.000) | 0.389 (0.000) | 0.337 (0.000) | −0.074 (0.180) | 1.396 (0.011) | 9.998 (0.265) | 0.257 |
| Pulp/Paper | 0.208[□] (0.000) | 0.087 (0.001) | 0.048 (0.070) | 0.029 (0.733) | 1.604 (0.001) | 10.83 (0.054) | 0.144 |
| Printing | 0.008 (0.958) | 0.192 (0.002) | 0.367 (0.000) | −0.073 (0.345) | 1.428 (0.056) | 16.37 (0.005) | 0.169 |
| Chemical | 0.293[□] (0.000) | 0.159 (0.000) | 0.284 (0.000) | −0.026 (0.664) | 1.984 (0.000) | 22.10 (0.001) | 0.280 |
| Rubber/Plastic | 0.280[□] (0.000) | 0.119 (0.000) | 0.269 (0.000) | 0.032 (0.505) | 3.461 (0.000) | 16.61 (0.000) | 0.341 |
| Stone/Mineral | 0.723[□] (0.000) | 0.138 (0.036) | 0.487 (0.000) | 0.025 (0.775) | 2.686 (0.000) | 73.48 (0.000) | 0.259 |
| Iron/Steel | 0.161 (0.210) | 0.095 (0.001) | 0.443 (0.000) | −0.048 (0.439) | 2.370 (0.000) | 40.76 (0.000) | 0.328 |
| Machinery | −0.084 (0.217) | 0.019 (0.558) | 0.498 (0.000) | −0.059 (0.437) | 3.047 (0.000) | 20.32 (0.002) | 0.287 |
| Electro | 0.010 (0.929) | 0.037 (0.393) | 0.434 (0.000) | 0.059 (0.528) | 1.939 (0.000) | 31.52 (0.000) | 0.248 |
| Motor vehicles | 0.611[□] (0.000) | 0.083 (0.009) | 0.309 (0.000) | 0.094 (0.043) | 1.619 (0.000) | 24.41 (0.000) | 0.196 |

Source: Brännlund et al., 2014

Note: [□] Indicates that EP is statistically more responsive to changes in the $CO_2$ tax compared to changes in the fossil fuel price.* If the *P*-value for the Hausman test is lower than 0.05, the fixed effects model is selected.

respectively. But EP is more sensitive to the tax. The cost share of fossil fuel also seems to be important for the development of EP, possibly because firms with substantial fuel use also have the most to gain from improving energy/fuel efficiency and thus EP. Capital intensity has a negative sign, but is not statistically significant.

Sector results exhibit similar pattern as aggregate results, but in some sectors the tax effect is not significant (Mining, Printing, Iron/Steel, Machinery, and Electro). Fuel price has a significant positive impact on EP across most sectors, which is in line with expectations. In the sectors where the tax is a statistically significant determinant of EP, it is more pronounced than the fuel price effect (except for Wood). This suggests a signaling effect connected to the tax. One interpretation of this effect is that an increase in the tax may be perceived as long-term, and at the same time it signals that $CO_2$ is a "bad" output, while fuel price changes are perceived as more short-term with the possibility of a swift change again, and therefore the response is comparatively moderate.

Higher fuel cost share is associated with a higher EP in all sectors, in line with the result for total manufacturing. Again, possibly because firms with high fuel usage have the most to gain from lowering fuel consumption and emissions. The effect on EP of capital intensity is statistically significant only in Mining and Motor vehicles, suggesting capital intensity is not an important determinant for EP in general.

Brännlund et al. (2014) show additional results for other parameters that we briefly summarize here. The size effect is positive, suggesting that bigger firms show relatively better EP, this effect is, however, only significant in some sectors. The time-trend effect is generally positive with either concave or convex shape. One interpretation of this result is that improvements in EP are stimulated by a trend-like increase in overall environmental awareness among firms and in society as a whole during the period studied. It can also be attributed to technological change, or a mix of both.

### 4.1.5 Conclusions: environmental performance and the $CO_2$ tax, 1990–2004

- During 1991 to 2004, the Swedish manufacturing industry improved EP 45 percent by reducing emission by 10 percent and increasing production by 35 percent.
- The evidence points to the $CO_2$ tax as a significant reason for this development.
- A tax on carbon is an efficient way to decarbonize the economy, and it may even dominate effects from increased fossil fuel prices.
- Furthermore, the results show that almost all sectors experienced falling emissions while production increased, i.e., we see absolute decoupling between production and emissions.
- The analysis indicates that EP in most sectors is more sensitive to the tax than to the fossil fuel price, referred to as a "signaling" effect; i.e., the tax signals negative properties of the taxed bad goods (fossil fuels).

## 4.2   Productivity, carbon prices, and incentives for technological progress: evidence from the pulp and paper industry, 1998–2008

The remainder of this chapter is devoted to the study presented in Lundgren et al. (2015). The questions asked in that study are similar to those in Brännlund et al. (2014), but the focus is on a different period (some overlapping) and one particular sector. Also, the performance measures are a conventional productivity indicator (not including bads) and an environmentally sensitive productivity indicator (including bads), the latter similar to the EP measure studied in Brännlund et al. (2014); they both have in common that reduction in bad outputs is credited.

There is concern that the carbon prices generated by climate policies are too low to create the incentives needed to stimulate technological development. Lundgren et al. (2015) empirically analyze how the Swedish carbon dioxide ($CO_2$) tax and the European Union emissions trading system (EU ETS) have affected productivity development in the Swedish pulp and paper industry during the period 1998 to 2008, and focus especially on technological development. First, a Luenberger total factor productivity (TFP) indicator, with its two components of technical efficiency change and technological development, is computed based on directional distance functions using data envelopment analysis (DEA). Second, the effect of climate policy on TFP is estimated using regression models. The approach of regressing DEA estimates of productivity on explanatory variables has been widely applied. Very few studies account for serial correlation in the productivity indicator. To account for this, Lundgren et al. (2015) follow Levine et al. (2000) and Zhengfei and Lansink (2006) and apply a system generalized method of moments (GMM) estimator.

TFP is computed both excluding and including emissions. A few studies have used this approach, see, e.g., Färe et al. (2001) and Chapter 3. TFP growth will be interpreted differently depending on whether emissions are included or not. Lundgren et al. (2015) take the analysis a step further by investigating whether the impact of climate and energy policies on TFP will be interpreted differently when excluding and including emissions, especially on the technological development component. Given that these types of policies lead to reduced emissions, the hypothesis is that they will have a larger impact on TFP when including emissions and crediting reduction of them.

Our results show that climate policy had a modest or no impact on technological development in the pulp and paper industry. If significant, it was negative, which would suggest that costs from policy outweigh the benefits. The price of fossil fuels (net of $CO_2$ tax), on the contrary, seems to have created important incentives for technological development. Hence, the results suggest that the carbon prices faced by the industry through EU ETS and the $CO_2$ tax may have been too low to create incentives for investments that spur technological development. When designing policy to mitigate $CO_2$ emissions, it is vital that the policy creates a carbon price that is high enough – otherwise the pressure on technological development will not be sufficiently strong.

### 4.2.1 The Luenberger productivity indicator

See Chapter 2, Section 2.4, for a detailed description of this productivity measure. Chapter 2 also discusses the production possibility set and its axioms and the directional distance function. Here we apply the output-oriented version of the Luenberger productivity indicator, which is composed of directional output distance functions representing the production technology of the pulp and paper firms in the study. The directional output distance function is a measure of technical inefficiency and measures the maximum expansion of the good output and contraction of bad outputs.

As defined in Chapter 2, the production technology is characterized by its output possibility set, $P(x)$, where $x$ is a vector of inputs, and the directional output distance function is defined on this set as:

$$\vec{D}o\left(x,y,b;g_y,g_b\right)=\max\left\{\beta:(y+\beta\cdot g_y,b-\beta\cdot g_b)\in P(x)\right\} \qquad (4.3)$$

The directional vector, $g=(g_y,g_b)$, describes how the output vector $(y,b)$ – good and bad output – is projected onto the technological frontier of the output possibility set. Given the directional vector $g$, the distance function simultaneously expands good outputs and contracts bad outputs. The function takes the value of zero for output vectors on the frontier and positive values for vectors below the frontier.

•Given Equation (4.3), the Luenberger indicator may be expressed as follows:

$$
\begin{aligned}
L_{t-1}^{t}\left(x,y,b;g_y,g_b\right)=\frac{1}{2}\Big[&\vec{D}_O^{t}\left(x^{t-1},y^{t-1},b^{t-1};g_y,g_b\right)\\
&-\vec{D}_O^{t}\left(x^{t},y^{t},b^{t};g_y,g_b\right)\\
&+\vec{D}_O^{t-1}\left(x^{t-1},y^{t-1},b^{t-1};g_y,g_b\right)\\
&-\vec{D}_O^{t-1}\left(x^{t},y^{t},b^{t};g_y,g_b\right)\Big]
\end{aligned}
\qquad (4.4)
$$

which relates firm productivity in adjacent periods, $t - 1$ and $t$. The two reference technologies $\vec{D}o^{t-1}$ and $\vec{D}o^{t}$ are constructed from period $t - 1$ and $t$ data, respectively. The input vector and the good and bad output vectors, $(x^{\tau}, y^{\tau}, b^{\tau})$, $\tau = t - 1$, and $t$, are compared with these technologies. The Luenberger productivity indicator takes positive values for positive changes between two years and negative values for negative changes.

The productivity change expression in Equation (4.4) can be decomposed into a technological change component,

$$LTCH_{t-1}^{t} = \frac{1}{2}\left[\vec{D}_{O}^{t}\left(x^{t}, y^{t}, b^{t}; g_{y}, g_{b}\right) - \vec{D}_{O}^{t-1}\left(x^{t}, y^{t}, b^{t}; g_{y}, g_{b}\right) \right.$$
$$\left. + \vec{D}_{O}^{t}\left(x^{t-1}, y^{t-1}, b^{t-1}; g_{y}, g_{b}\right) - \vec{D}_{O}^{t-1}\left(x^{t-1}, y^{t-1}, b^{t-1}; g_{y}, g_{b}\right)\right] \tag{4.5}$$

and a technical efficiency change component,

$$LECH_{t-1}^{t} = \vec{D}_{O}^{t-1}\left(x^{t-1}, y^{t-1}, b^{t-1}; g_{y}, g_{b}\right) - \vec{D}_{O}^{t}\left(x^{t}, y^{t}, b^{t}; g_{y}, g_{b}\right) \tag{4.6}$$

Equation (4.5) measures the positive, neutral, or negative shifts in the frontier of the output possibility set, $P(x)$, and the expression in Equation (4.6) indicates changes in the distance to the frontier.

So far bad outputs, $b$, have been included in the calculations. In the empirical application, the Luenberger productivity indicator is also computed excluding bad outputs. For details on the Luenberger indicator that excludes bad outputs, see Chapter 3. The difference is basically that a few restrictions in the DEA computation of the distance functions (see below) are omitted.

### 4.2.2   Pulp and paper industry data, 1998–2008

The impacts of climate policy on the productivity of the Swedish pulp and paper firms are assessed using firm-level data collected and supplied by Statistics Sweden (www.scb.se), covering the period 1998–2008. Firms produce one good output, which is derived by dividing the sales value at the firm level by a sector-level producer price index. By-products are three bad outputs measured in tons – carbon dioxide ($CO_2$), sulfur dioxide ($SO_2$), and nitrogen oxide ($NO_x$). Inputs are the capital stock in MSEK, the number of employees, fossil fuels (coal, oil, natural gas, and propane), and non-fossil fuels (electricity, biofuels, and heat) in MWh. The observed good and bad outputs and input quantities are used to compute the Luenberger productivity indicators.

The variables $ctax_{kt}$ and $etax_{kt}$ capture $CO_2$ and energy taxes in SEK/kWh paid by the firms, and $pff_{kt}$ reflects the variation in the price of fossil fuels (derived from fuel use and fuel cost). In total, we have an unbalanced panel of 1,006 observations from 1998 to 2008. Descriptive statistics are summarized in Table 4.3.

About 16 percent of greenhouse gas emissions from industrial combustion are generated from the pulp and paper industry (Ministry of the Environment, 2009). However, this industry has undertaken a shift from fossil fuels to biofuels. Table 4.3 shows clearly that non-fossil fuels are a significant energy source. The average energy tax payment was low during the period. One reason for this is that the industry paid no tax on electricity use in production until 2004. Since then, the tax rate has been 0.005 SEK/kWh, which is in line with the EU minimum requirements. Furthermore, in 2005, a voluntary program for improving energy efficiency in energy intensive industries (PFE) was introduced, allowing partaking plants to be exempt from the energy tax on electricity, which also contributed to a lower average tax payment.

Figure 4.4 illustrates how the effective $CO_2$ tax rate and the fossil fuel price developed over the period studied and also including the years 1995–2007.

In real terms, the $CO_2$ tax has increased marginally while the price of fossil fuels has increased substantially.

The ETS variables are calculated based on monthly price data in euro per ton. The average prices in 2005, 2006, 2007, and 2008 were SEK 0.0604, 0.0448, 0.0016, and 0.0505 per kWh. The EUR/SEK exchange rate 2005–2008 was on average approximately EUR 1 = SEK 9. The relatively low

*Table 4.3* Descriptive statistics, the Swedish pulp and paper industry 1998–2008. Base year 2008

| Variables | Units | Mean | SD | Minimum | Maximum |
|---|---|---|---|---|---|
| Output | MSEK | 1086.305 | 1734.428 | 9.470 | 14042.553 |
| $CO_2$ | ton | 21741.938 | 37578.105 | 1.065 | 236158.894 |
| $SO_2$ | ton | 32.760 | 62.205 | 0.000 | 448.842 |
| $NO_x$ | ton | 53.665 | 98.442 | 0.001 | 541.763 |
| Capital | MSEK | 858.789 | 1462.879 | 2.152 | 8203.496 |
| Labor | Workers | 422.404 | 597.908 | 9.000 | 5869.000 |
| Fossil fuels | MWh | 81028.227 | 138289.775 | 3.984 | 862354.130 |
| Non-fossil fuels | MWh | 415054.457 | 844452.090 | 36.000 | 5588577.756 |
| $CO_2$ tax | SEK/kWh | 0.041 | 0.188 | 0.000 | 2.611 |
| Energy tax | SEK/kWh | 0.001 | 0.002 | 0.000 | 0.033 |
| Fossil fuel price | SEK/kWh | 0.417 | 0.221 | 0.101 | 1.904 |
| Non-fossil fuel price | SEK/kWh | 0.352 | 0.178 | 0.044 | 1.044 |

Source: Lundgren et al., 2015

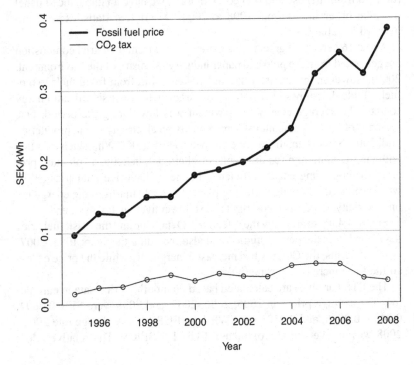

*Figure 4.4* Fossil fuel price and $CO_2$ tax, 1995–2008. Base year 2008.
Source: Lundgren et al., 2015

price per kWh in 2007 is explained by the fact that this was the last year of the first trading period and allowances could not be saved for the next trading period. The price volatilities in kWh were calculated from monthly prices, as the standard deviations of the average prices above, and are correspondingly 0.0003, 0.0014, 0.0002, and 0.0016.

### 4.2.3   Estimating the Luenberger indicator and econometric approach

The directional distance functions that make up the Luenberger indicator in Equation (4.4) are computed using data envelopment analysis, DEA (again, see Chapter 2 for more details on DEA). The directional vector $g$ credits simultaneous expansion of good outputs and contraction of bad outputs, and when solving the maximization problems we explicitly assume a common direction for all observations, i.e., $g = (1, -1)$. Producing a single good output and a single bad output the maximization problem for, e.g., $\vec{D}_o^t(t-1)$ is then, for observations $(x^{k'}, y^{k'}, b^{k'})$ and $k' = 1,...,K$ firms:

$$\vec{D}_o^t\left(x^{k't-1}, y^{k't-1}, b^{k't-1}; 1, -1\right) = \max_{z_k, \beta} \beta$$

s.t.

(i) $\displaystyle\sum_{k=1}^{K} z_k^t y_k^t \geq y_{k'}^{t-1} + \beta \cdot 1$

(ii) $\displaystyle\sum_{k=1}^{K} z_k^t b_k^t = b_{k'}^{t-1} - \beta \cdot 1$

(iii) $\displaystyle\sum_{k=1}^{K} z_k^t x_{kn}^t \leq x_{k'n}^{t-1}, \qquad n = 1,...,N$ \hfill (4.7)

(iv) $z_k^t \geq 0, \qquad k = 1,...,K$

(v) $\displaystyle\sum_{j=1}^{J} b_{kj} > 0, \qquad k = 1,...,K$

(vi) $\displaystyle\sum_{k=1}^{K} b_{kj} > 0, \qquad j = 1,...,J$

Constraints (i) and (ii) impose the axioms of the good output being strongly disposable and the good and bad outputs being together weakly disposable. Inputs being strongly disposable are modeled by constraint (iii), and constraint (iv) imposes constant returns to scale. Furthermore, null-jointness holds when the data fulfill constraints (v) and (vi). The other three distance functions are computed correspondingly using the same technique.

Note that bad output is modeled as a single variable in terms of a bad output index (BOI) consisting of the weighted mean of $CO_2$, $SO_2$, and $NO_x$, i.e., $BOI = \sum_j b_j \cdot (b_j / \sum_j b_j), j = CO_2, SO_2, NO_x$. To avoid problems with infeasible solutions, all the variables in the estimations are mean normalized, i.e., $x_{kn}^t / \bar{x}_n$, $y_k^t / \bar{y}$, and $BOI_k^t / \overline{BOI}$, where the "bar" denotes the mean of the variable. We now move on to the econometric specification.

Following Levine et al. (2000) and Zhengfei and Lansink (2006), a GMM (generalized method of moments) estimator originally developed for dynamic models of panel data is used to estimate the effects of climate policy on firms' productivity change rates. By construction, the Luenberger productivity indicator generates productivity change rates that are negatively serially correlated over years. A high change rate in the current period will suppress the potential for productivity growth in the next period. Contrary to the Luenberger indicator used in Lundgren et al. (2015), Zhengfei and Lansink (2006) employ a Malmquist productivity index and stress the significance of accounting for negative serial correlation. See Lundgren et al. (2015) for details on the econometric approach.

To estimate the effect of climate policy on total factor productivity, technological development, and technical efficiency change, as specified above, the system GMM dynamic panel data approach is used. That is, for $\zeta_{kt} = L^t_{k,t-1}, LTCH^t_{k,t-1}$, or $LECH^t_{k,t-1}$, the econometric model is as follows:

$$\zeta_{kt} = \alpha \zeta_{k,t-1} + \beta_1 ctax_{kt} + \beta_2 etax_{kt} + \beta_5 pff_{kt} + \beta_6 R\&D_{kt}$$
$$+ \beta_7 D_{pulp} + \beta_8 D_{paper} + \beta_9 Trend + \eta_k + v_{kt} \tag{4.8}$$

The lag, $\zeta_{k,t-1}$, accounts for the intertemporal negative serial correlation problem. The parameter $\alpha$ is therefore expected to have a negative sign.

Variables capturing Swedish climate policy are analyzed in terms of the $CO_2$ tax, $ctax_{kt}$, and the energy tax, $etax_{kt}$. The EU ETS is captured by $pETS_{kt}$, i.e., the yearly average price of allowances, and $pETSvol_{kt}$, i.e., the volatility of the ETS price. The impacts of these variables are not obvious. Since a positive change means higher costs for the firm, it would be expected to have a negative effect. But policy changes may spur investments in new environmentally friendly and/or energy saving technology, which in the end could enhance technological progress and productivity (according to the so-called Porter hypothesis). The empirical application will give us answers.

Moreover, a number of control variables are included. The variable $pff_{kt}$ denotes the price of fossil fuels, and its impact on $\zeta_{kt}$ is ambiguous for the same reasons as the policy variables. The variable $R\&D$ is modeled as a dummy variable capturing if firms have costs for R&D (in this case related to environmental protection). Fischer and Newell (2008) claim that R&D efforts could be a complement to price-setting policy measures and therefore could have a positive effect in the long run. However, since it is here modeled in a static setting (short run), we expect a negative impact on $\zeta_{kt}$. The dummies $D_{pulp}$ and $D_{paper}$ denote pulp and paper firms, respectively, and capture differences compared with respect to firm types. The *Trend* variable takes into account a possible trend in productivity development.

The error term, $\varepsilon_{kt} = \eta_k + v_{kt}$, consists of an unobservable individual firm effect, $\eta_k$, and a random disturbance, $v_{kt}$. The parameters estimated by the model are $\alpha$, and $\beta_1, ..., \beta_9$.

### 4.2.4   Results: total factor productivity and its components and the effects of climate policy, 1998–2008

The estimated Luenberger indicator results in measures of total factor productivity change, technological development, and technical efficiency change (here expressed as relative to output): $L^t_{t-1}/y^{t-1}$, $LTCH^t_{t-1}/y^{t-1}$, and

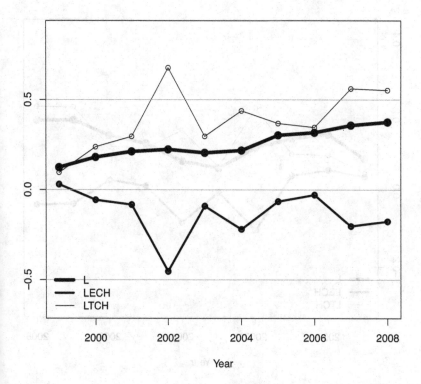

*Figure 4.5* Productivity growth – excluding emissions
Source: Lundgren et al., 2015

$LECH_{t-1}^{t}/y^{t-1}$. Figures 4.5 and 4.6 display the pulp and paper firms' development of total factor productivity and its components.

Productivity grew primarily due to technological development, irrespective of including or excluding emissions in the productivity measurement. Also, productivity growth is higher when ignoring emissions and this result is statistically significant, which indicates emissions have not been falling during the period studied. The result in Chapter 3 also presents similar result for the Swedish pulp and paper industry using a Luenberger approach, but for the longer period 1990–2008. However, in Chapter 3, for manufacturing as a whole (12 sectors), it was found that the estimated productivity growth is higher when including emissions, reflecting the downward trend in overall emissions. Färe et al. (2001) and Weber and Domazlicky (2001) also find that the estimated productivity growth in US state-level manufacturing is higher when including emissions.

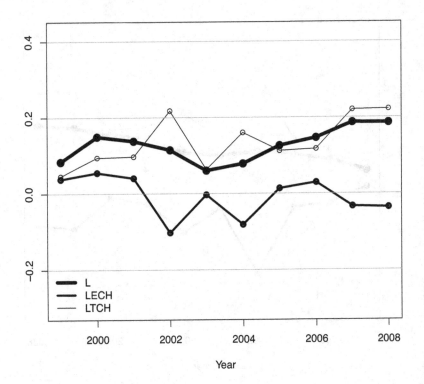

*Figure 4.6* Productivity growth – including emissions

Source: Lundgren et al., 2015

Results from the system GMM estimation of Equation (4.8) are provided in Tables 4.4 (emissions excluded) and 4.5 (emissions included). The AR(2) test shows no evidence of serial correlation. However, the Sargan test reveals that there are over-identifying restrictions in the equation for technological development when ignoring emissions in productivity measurement. This implies that the estimates for LTCH (technological change) may be inconsistent. Furthermore, the results in the tables show that there are no weak instrument problems producing biased estimates, as the absolute values of the estimates for the lagged $z$-variable are smaller than $|{-}0.80|$ (Bun and Windmeijer, 2010).

We now make some selected comments on the results.

When emissions are excluded, i.e., "conventional" productivity, the $CO_2$ tax has a positive effect on total factor productivity, which is driven mostly by positive technical efficiency during the period studied. This is not in line with the results in Lundgren and Marklund (2015) and results presented in

*Table 4.4* Policy effects on productivity – excluding emissions

| Dependent variable: $z_t$ | | Sample period: 1999–2008 (90 firms) | |
|---|---|---|---|
| Independent variable | L | LTCH | LECH |
| $z_{t-1}$ | −0.1098* | −0.3189*** | −0.186*** |
| | (−1.7297) | (−8.5433) | (−3.2231) |
| $CO_2$ tax | 0.5483** | −0.0958 | 0.4443*** |
| | (2.1296) | (−0.3807) | (2.6741) |
| Energy tax | 1.2171 | −3.8492 | 4.1804 |
| | (0.2114) | (−0.9388) | (0.7436) |
| ETS price | 1.412* | −2.4989*** | 4.487*** |
| | (1.8239) | (−4.2579) | (3.7475) |
| ETS price volatility | −4.3529* | −1.5149 | −2.8134 |
| | (−1.9115) | (−1.0382) | (−0.9762) |
| Fossil fuel price | 0.1449 | 0.1297*** | 0.0781 |
| | (1.3245) | (3.7175) | (0.5231) |
| R&D cost | −0.0183 | −0.1495* | −0.0345 |
| | (−0.8483) | (−1.6854) | (−1.4166) |
| Pulp firm | 0.01 | −0.0276 | −0.0248 |
| | (0.3094) | (−0.8233) | (−0.5378) |
| Paper firm | 0.0169 | −0.0313 | −0.0207 |
| | (0.5807) | (−0.7533) | (−0.8096) |
| Time | −0.005 | −0.0033 | −0.0131 |
| | (−0.683) | (−0.108) | (−1.1927) |
| Sargan test chisq(df = 52) | 55.7253 | 76.3092 | 63.1919 |
| *p*-value | 0.3365 | 0.0197 | 0.1375 |
| AR(2) Statistic | −0.4658 | −0.5021 | 0.6071 |
| *p*-value | 0.3207 | 0.3078 | 0.2719 |
| No. of observations | 1006 | 1006 | 1006 |

Source: Lundgren et al., 2015

Notes: *t*-values in parenthesis. *, **, and *** represent significance at the 10%, 5%, and 1% levels, respectively. Sargan is a test of the overidentifying restrictions. L: total factor productivity; LECH: efficiency change; LTCH: technological change.

Chapter 5, where a negative impact of $CO_2$ taxation on the profit technical efficiency level is found in the pulp and paper industry for the different period 1990–2004. Also, again for the period 1990–2004, Brännlund and Lundgren (2010) find that technological development in the Swedish manufacturing sector is independent of, or slows down due to, the $CO_2$ tax.

*Table 4.5* Policy effects on productivity – including emissions

| Dependent variable: $z_t$ | | Sample period: 1999–2008 (74 firms) | |
| --- | --- | --- | --- |
| Independent variable | L | LTCH | LECH |
| $z_{t-1}$ | −0.1257 | −0.3487*** | −0.2207*** |
| | (−1.6336) | (−7.1457) | (−3.012) |
| $CO_2$ tax | 0.0774 | −0.0042 | 0.0665 |
| | (1.3252) | (−0.2365) | (1.1338) |
| Energy tax | 8.5839 | −0.2604 | 7.5272 |
| | (1.2305) | (−0.0703) | (1.0782) |
| ETS price | 1.2319 | −0.7116** | 2.3186*** |
| | (1.3934) | (−2.4492) | (2.9222) |
| ETS price volatility | −3.2876 | −0.8968 | −2.5555 |
| | (−1.2659) | (−1.3952) | (−1.151) |
| Fossil fuel price | 0.0941 | −0.0533 | 0.1884 |
| | (0.8475) | (−1.557) | (1.2274) |
| R&D cost | −0.0596*** | −0.0079 | −0.0455 |
| | (−2.7851) | (−0.4012) | (−1.56) |
| Pulp firm | 0.0209 | 0.0368 | 0.0027 |
| | (0.6218) | (1.0971) | (0.0831) |
| Paper firm | 0.0443* | 0.0241** | 0.0426* |
| | (1.9454) | (2.2189) | (1.7423) |
| Time | −0.0058 | 0.0073** | −0.0173 |
| | (−0.6497) | (2.2308) | (−1.4859) |
| Sargan test chisq(df = 52) | 55.5276 | 61.7971 | 57.1289 |
| *p*-value | 0.3433 | 0.143 | 0.2904 |
| AR(2) Statistic | 0.2549 | 0.9045 | −0.2533 |
| *p*-value | 0.3994 | 0.1829 | 0.4 |
| No. of observations | 764 | 764 | 764 |

Source: Lundgren et al., 2015

Notes: *t*-values in parenthesis. *, **, and *** represent significance at the 10%, 5%, and 1% levels, respectively. Sargan is a test of the overidentifying restrictions. L: total factor productivity; LECH: efficiency change; LTCH: technological change.

When emissions are included in our analysis, "eco"-efficiency, however, the $CO_2$ tax has no effect on the productivity measures, contradicting Brännlund et al. (2014) (the study referred to earlier in this chapter), who find that EP, also a measure that credits simultaneous production increase and emission decrease, is significantly and positively correlated with the $CO_2$ tax.

The EU ETS price has a positive effect on technical efficiency change and a negative effect on technological change, regardless of whether emissions are included in the productivity measure. This is in line with the results by Commins et al. (2011), who find that the effect of EU ETS on technological progress is negative.

The Swedish EPA sent out a questionnaire in April 2006 to all Swedish plants included in EU ETS (Swedish EPA, 2007). One finding was that the share of plants inactive in EU ETS was large. Two-thirds responded that they had been allocated enough emission allowances to operate in an unchanged manner. So there was no need for them to take any measures during the period 2005–2007. The most common strategy to handle a deficit in allowances was to reduce emissions internally and not to buy emission allowances. What we see in the analysis in Lundgren et al. (2015) is that the EU ETS motivates firms to use the technologies and inputs at hand more efficiently; the EU ETS shows a positive effect on technical efficiency change.

The EU ETS price volatility has a negative impact on TFP growth when emissions are excluded. This confirms the general view that firms need stable long-term incentives in order to invest.

The energy tax has no significant impact regardless of whether emissions are included in the TFP measure. A likely explanation for this is that the energy taxes have been too low to have effect. This supports the result by Martin et al. (2009), who find no impact of the UK energy tax on employment, gross output, or TFP.

The price of fossil fuels has a positive effect on technological development when emissions are excluded from the estimations. However, when emissions are included in the estimations ("eco"-productivity), the price of fossil fuels has a neutral effect on the productivity measures, a result that differs from the study described in the first half of this chapter, Brännlund et al. (2014), where EP was positively and significantly affected by fossil fuel price in most sectors.

Overall, the results indicate that climate policy has had a modest impact on technological development in the pulp and paper industry, and if significant it has been negative. Productivity growth during 1998–2008 was mainly due to technological development, and we find that productivity growth was generally due to factors other than environmental (economic) policy instruments, e.g., the fossil fuel price seems to have been a more important factor.

If excluding or including emissions in the TFP measure leads to different policy recommendations, it is not obvious. The results indicate that the effect of climate policies on productivity, efficiency, and technological change works in the same direction irrespective of whether emissions are included. However, there is a tendency for climate policies to have less impact when emission reduction is credited in the productivity measurement, a result counterintuitive given that policy should induce emission reductions.

One possible root of the problem may be the amount of infeasible solutions when including bads; 24 percent of the firms are dismissed. A logit model indicates that excluded observations are relatively fossil fuel intensive. Descriptive statistics, divided into infeasible and feasible observations, also indicate that the average $CO_2$ tax payment was more than three times higher for infeasible than for feasible observations. Also, including emissions to TFP computations adds restrictions to the optimization problem. More firms will be operating on the frontier with less variation in absolute technical efficiency scores. Hence, the variation in technological development and efficiency change will also be smaller (see Figure 4.6). This can potentially explain why the $CO_2$ tax and the price of fossil fuels have less impact on productivity development when adding bad output to the TFP measure.

Finally, there is no obvious answer to the question of whether to include emissions or not when computing TFP. Firstly, it depends on whose perspective is in focus. From the pure firm perspective, emissions can be excluded. From a societal point of view, however, they should be included (see discussion and results in Chapter 3). Secondly, as shown in this paper, there are also issues of methodological nature (infeasible solutions) to take into account.

### 4.2.5    Conclusions: total factor productivity and its components and the effects of climate policy, 1998–2008

- There is a general concern that carbon prices have been too low to create incentives for technological development.
- Lundgren et al. (2015) study the effects of carbon and energy taxes and EU ETS on total factor productivity and its two components of technical efficiency change and technological development in the pulp and paper industry.
- The results indicate that climate policy has had a modest impact on technological development in the pulp and paper industry, and if significant it has been negative.
- This confirms the concern of too-low carbon prices. That high energy prices can affect technological development is apparent from looking at the fossil fuel price, which has had a positive effect on technological development. The increase in the price of fossil fuels has been larger than the change in carbon and energy taxes in Sweden.
- When designing policy towards mitigating $CO_2$ emissions, it is vital that the policy creates a carbon price that is high enough – otherwise the motivation to invest in green technologies and the pressure on technological development will not be amply strong.

## 4.3 References

Azar, C., J. Holmberg, S. Karlsson, 2002. Decoupling – Past Trends and Prospects for the Future. Report for the Environmental Advisory Council. Edita Norstedts, Stockholm, Sweden.

Brännlund, R., T. Lundgren, 2010. Environmental Policy and Profitability – Evidence from Swedish Industry. *Environmental Economics and Policy Studies* 12: 59–78.

Brännlund, R., T. Lundgren, P-O. Marklund, 2014. Carbon Intensity in Production and the Effects of Climate Policy – Evidence from Swedish Industry. *Energy Policy* 67: 844–857.

Bun, M.J.G., F. Windmeijer, 2010. The Weak Instrument Problem of the System GMM Estimator in Dynamic Panel Data Models. *Econometrics Journal* 13: 95–126.

Commins, N., S. Lyons, M. Schiffbauer, R. Tol, 2011. Climate Policy and Corporate Behavior. *Energy Journal* 32: 51–68.

Dinda, S., 2004. Environmental Kuznets Curve Hypothesis: A Survey. *Ecological Economics* 49: 431–455.

Färe, R., S. Grosskopf, C.A. Pasurka, Jr., 2001. Accounting for Air Pollution Emissions in Measures of State Manufacturing Productivity Growth. *Journal of Regional Science* 41: 381–409.

Färe, R., S. Grosskopf, C.A. Pasurka, Jr., 2006. Social Responsibility: U.S. Power Plants 1985–1998. *Journal of Productivity Analysis* 26: 259–267.

Fischer, C., R.G. Newell, 2008. Environmental and Technology Policies for Climate Mitigation. *Journal of Environmental Economics and Management* 55: 142–162.

Grossman, G.M., A.B. Krueger, 1995. Economic Growth and the Environment. *Quarterly Journal of Economics* 110: 353–377.

Levine, R., N. Loayza, T. Beck, 2000. Financial Intermediation and Growth: Causality and Causes. *Journal of Monetary Economics* 46: 31–77.

Lundgren, T., P-O. Marklund, 2015. Climate Policy, Environmental Performance, and Profits. *Journal of Productivity Analysis* 44(3): 225–235.

Lundgren, T., P-O. Marklund, E. Samakovlis, W. Zhou, 2015. Carbon Prices and Incentives for Technological Development. *Journal of Environmental Management* 150: 393–403.

Martin, R., L.B. de Preux, U.J. Wagner, 2009. The Impacts of the Climate Change Levy on Business: Evidence from Microdata. CEP Discussion Paper No. 917. London School of Economics and Political Science, London, United Kingdom.

Ministry of the Environment, 2009. Sweden's Fifth National Communication on Climate Change. Ds 2009: 63.

Swedish EPA, 2007. Corporate Strategies for Emission Trading and Climate Commitments – A Survey of Corporate Behavior and Attitudes in the Context of the EU-ETS. Report 5679 (in Swedish, Summary in English).

Tyteca, D., 1996. On the Measurement of Environmental Performance of Firms – A Literature Review. *Journal of Environmental Management* 46: 281–308.

Weber, W.L., B. Domazlicky, 2001. Productivity Growth and Pollution in State Manufacturing. *Review of Economics and Statistics* 83: 195–199.

Zhengfei, G., A.O. Lansink, 2006. The Source of Productivity Growth in Dutch Agriculture: A Perspective from Finance. *American Journal of Agricultural Economics* 88: 644–656.

Zhou, P., B.W. Ang, K.L. Poh, 2008. A Survey of Data Envelopment Analysis in Energy and Environmental Studies. *European Journal of Operational Research* 189: 1–18.

# 5 The Swedish CO₂ tax, environmental performance, and impact on profits

## A stochastic frontier analysis

This chapter looks more closely on the impacts on profits of climate policy – here in the form of a $CO_2$ tax – and environmental performance (EP). Results from two studies using the same methodology and data set are reported. The method used is stochastic frontier analysis (SFA) and more specifically we assess profit efficiency. We start by gauging how the $CO_2$ tax directly affects profit efficiency, an analysis that addresses the so-called strong form of the Porter hypothesis; the right type of policy instruments can lessen the cost of regulation or even neutralize it. Then we go on to add a link to the chain between policy and profits, $CO_2$ emissions performance or EP. That is, we assess how the $CO_2$ tax affects EP, and how EP potentially affects profits. The latter analysis pertains both to the Porter hypothesis and the so-called corporate social responsibility (CSR) literature; i.e., EP can be motivated by external (Porter) and/or internal (CSR) policy, which both potentially have an impact on profits. The main presentation in this chapter will be focused on the modeling and estimation of the $CO_2$ tax and its direct impact on profit efficiency. The modeling and estimation approach in the second study, where we add EP to the mix, is identical; it is only the inefficiency part of the model that differs.

## 5.1 The CO₂ tax and impact on profits

One common argument against environmental regulations is that they may, in addition to simply increasing costs, hamper productivity and competitiveness among firms, and therefore further reduce profits. Viewed from this perspective, the environmental ambitions of the EU and Sweden may have far-reaching negative effects on the regulated companies to compete in international markets. On the other hand, the well-known Porter hypothesis (Porter, 1991; Porter and van der Linde, 1995) claims that introducing, or strengthening, the "right kind" of regulation (economic incentives, such as taxes and tradable permits) will induce productivity gains and reduce inefficiencies, leading to increased competitiveness and profits. Environmental policy could therefore be costless and, by being an early mover, the EU and Sweden could actually benefit from climate mitigation.

The main purpose is to assess the contemporary and dynamic effects of the Swedish CO$_2$ tax scheme on firm profit efficiency in the manufacturing industry during the years 1990 to 2004. Firms' efficiency may differ due to heterogeneity in production technologies and differences in management of the production processes. The theoretical profit efficiency approach adopted is based on Kumbhakar and Lovell (2000) and Kumbhakar (2001), and efficiency scores are empirically estimated by using a SFA approach suggested by Battese and Coelli (1995) (simultaneously estimating the profit frontier and explaining variation in efficiency). We explicitly apply profit efficiency, modeled as a constant multiple of technical efficiency, as a measure on how efficiently energy inputs are used in production.

Broberg et al. (2013) also analyze the contemporary and temporal effects of environmental regulation on technical efficiency in Swedish manufacturing. They use environmental protection investment as a proxy for regulation stringency and test for effects on production technical efficiency. The results indicate that regulation causes efficiency losses in the five studied Swedish industries during 1999–2004. However, using investments in environmental protection as a proxy for regulation stringency may be problematic. For instance, as investments may be voluntary, environmental investments do not necessarily reflect regulation stringency. The analysis in this study covers more industries over a longer period, 1990–2004, and, above all, the regulation stringency is measured by CO$_2$ taxes actually paid by firms. Furthermore, in our analysis we focus explicitly on profit efficiency, which from a Porter perspective is appropriate, and not production efficiency as in Broberg et al. (2013).

### 5.1.1   The Porter hypothesis

Brännlund and Lundgren (2009) and Ambec et al. (2013) provide overviews of theoretical and empirical findings concerning the Porter hypothesis. The hypothesis may be found valid in certain circumstances, e.g., when there are other market imperfections in addition to the environmental problems. However, even though theoretical studies may give important insights, the task of validating the Porter hypothesis is mainly an empirical one. In this context, Jaffe and Palmer (1997) separate the hypothesis into a weak, narrow, and strong version. The weak version only alludes to environmental regulation stimulating profit-maximizing firms to certain types of innovations. Whether these innovations are socially beneficial or not is ignored. The narrow version refers to economic instruments giving maximizing firms greater incentive to innovate compared to command-and-control instruments. Finally, the strong version assumes that firms are not necessarily maximizing profits, and that environmental regulation therefore will make them discover profit potentials and induce them to improve economic performance. Therefore, the strong version of the Porter hypothesis is associated with a "win-win" outcome, improving both the environment and firms' performance and competitiveness. Lanoie et al. (2011) observe two different types of empirical studies: (a) Studies that test the weak version of the Porter hypothesis by addressing the impact of environmental regulation on firms' innovation and choice of technology, measured by different types of investments; and (b) studies testing the strong version of the hypothesis by addressing the impact on firms' economic performance, e.g., productivity. Lanoie et al. (2011) is the first study trying to test all the three versions of the Porter hypothesis, including also the narrow version. Generally, they find strong support for the weak version and, as they put it, "qualified" support for the narrow version (p. 837). However, no support for the strong version of the Porter hypothesis is found. Other studies focusing explicitly on the strong version are Managi et al. (2005), Lanoie et al. (2008), and Broberg et al. (2013), and together they provide findings that are not conclusive. However, uniquely, these studies have in common that they consider temporal dynamics when estimating the effects of environmental policy on different types of economic performance. The dynamic perspective is most crucial to the Porter hypothesis.

In this study, the strong version of the Porter hypothesis is tested. In contrast to earlier studies, the contribution to this particular type of studies is as follows: (1) We use a unique data set, which includes total $CO_2$ taxes actually paid at the firm level in Swedish industry (the $CO_2$ tax being an economic instrument in accordance with the narrow version of the Porter hypothesis); (2) contemporaneous and dynamic effects of $CO_2$ taxation on firms' economic performance are estimated; and (3) economic performance is measured by profit efficiency.

### 5.1.2  Profit efficiency

The Porter hypothesis argues that firms' performances are positively affected by environmental regulation. Performance may be measured in terms of efficiency in production, and efficiency is typically decomposed into a technical and an allocative component. However, in testing the Porter hypothesis, which explicitly focuses on the effects on firms' private economic performance, our interest is primarily on the effects on firms' technical efficiency, related to the use of a given input mix in production. Therefore, from the firm's private point of view, we assume allocative efficiency in production.

Technical efficiency is commonly analyzed in a primal setting by specifying and estimating production functions. However, as pointed out by Kumbhakar (2001), there are some estimation issues related to this particular approach. For instance, regressors are assumed exogenous in estimations, but in neoclassical theory inputs are treated as endogenous in firms' optimization behavior. Consequently, estimating primal production functions with inputs as regressors may lead to inconsistent parameter and efficiency estimates. This problem is avoided when analyzing technical efficiency in a dual setting, e.g., by specifying and estimating profit functions. For a general description of the concept of profit efficiency, see Section 2.5 in Chapter 2.

Our main purpose is to estimate profit frontiers and profit technical efficiency scores, and then to test whether the variation in efficiency depends on $CO_2$ tax rates. The estimations are based on a single-equation method, and the primary reason for adopting such a method is that it allows for a fairly straightforward single-stage estimating procedure. Alternatively, the profit frontier and efficiency scores are estimated in a first stage, and then in a second stage, separately from the first, efficiency is regressed on a set of exogenously given firm-specific variables. However, running the estimations in two separate stages requires contradictory assumptions. Efficient parameter estimates of the profit frontier and profit efficiency require that efficiency is identically distributed in the first stage. However, the second stage requires the opposite assumption. Coelli (1996): "The two-stage estimation procedure is unlikely to provide estimates which are as efficient as those that could be obtained using a single-stage estimation procedure".

We use a stochastic frontier analysis approach within a single-stage estimating framework, which was suggested by Battese and Coelli (1995). Recent studies using the single-stage framework have been reported by, e.g., van der Vlist et al. (2007) and Shadbegian and Gray (2006), although both estimate production functions and not profit functions.

The stochastic profit frontier model is expressed as:

$$\ln\left(\pi^{kt}(pe^{-u},w,q)\right) = \ln\left(\pi^{kt}(p,w,q;\alpha)\right) + v^{kt} - u^{kt} \tag{5.1}$$

where $\pi^{kt}(pe^{-u},w,q)$ is the observed profit of firm $k$ in year $t$, and $\pi^{kt}(p,w,q)$ represents the deterministic part of the profit frontier. The error term is divided into two components $v^{kt}$ and $u^{kt}$. Introducing the stochastic part of the frontier, the component $v^{kt}$ arises from random shocks and measurement errors, and these influences are $iid\,N(0,\sigma_v^2)$ and independent of $u^{kt}$, which is a nonnegative random variable that captures technical inefficiency, and is independently (not identically) distributed such that it is obtained by truncation at zero of $N(z^{kt}\delta,\sigma_u^2)$. If the OLS residuals of the expression in Equation (5.1) are negatively skewed, it indicates technical inefficiency, i.e., $u^{kt} > 0$ (Kumbhakar and Lovell, 2000). Finally, $\sigma_v^2$ and $\sigma_u^2$ are replaced with $\sigma^2 = \sigma_v^2 + \sigma_u^2$ and $\gamma = \sigma_u^2/(\sigma_v^2 + \sigma_u^2)$.[1]

Technical inefficiency in Equation (5.1) is defined as:

$$u^{kt} = z^{kt}\delta + v^{kt} \tag{5.2}$$

where $z^{kt} = [z_1^{kt}, ..., z_j^{kt}]$ is a vector of variables that potentially have an effect on efficiency, and $\delta$ is a vector of parameters to be estimated. The random variable, $v^{kt} \sim N(0, \sigma_v^2)$, is truncated by the variable truncation point $-z^{kt}\delta = v^{kt} - u^{kt}$.

Profit technical inefficiency is then defined as:

$$-u^{\pi, kt} = -\rho \cdot u^{kt} \tag{5.3}$$

where $\rho = 1/(1-r)$, and $u^{\pi, kt}$ is to be interpreted as firm $k$'s percentage profit loss in period $t$ caused by producing output technically inefficient (Kumbhakar, 2001). Equation (5.3) shows that profit technical inefficiency is a constant multiple of technical inefficiency, and the profit frontier, $\pi(p, w, q)$, is a neutral transformation of the observed profit function, $\pi(pe^{-u}, w, q)$, which means that shifts of the profit function are independent of prices (Kumbhakar, 2001). This follows from the underlying technology being homogenous of degree $r$ in inputs.

Finally, profit technical efficiency is expressed as:

$$PE^{kt} = \exp\left(-u^{\pi, kt}\right) = \exp\left(-\rho u^{kt}\right) = \exp\left(-\rho\left(z^{kt}\delta - v^{kt}\right)\right) \tag{5.4}$$

which shows that the smaller the nonnegative profit inefficiency variable, $u^{\pi, kt}$, the more profit efficient is firm $k$ at time $t$. Hence, when $u^{\pi, kt} = 0$, then $PE^{kt} = 1$ and the firm is operating efficiently on the technology frontier. The likelihood function of the model is provided in Appendix 5.

### 5.1.3   *Empirical approach*

For estimating purposes, equation (5.1) is parameterized as a Translog flexible functional form. Specifically, for firm $k$ in period $t$, in the case of a single output and a single quasi-fixed input, the econometric expression of the variable profit function is:

$$\begin{aligned}
\ln\left(\pi^{kt}(pe^{-u}, w, q)\right) = {} & \alpha_0 + \gamma_q \ln q^{kt} + \alpha_p \ln p^{kt} + \sum_{n=1}^{N} \alpha_n \ln w_n^{kt} \\
& + \frac{1}{2}\gamma_{qq}(\ln q^{kt})^2 + \eta_{qp} \ln q^{kt} \ln p^{kt} + \sum_{n=1}^{N} \eta_{qn} \ln q^{kt} \ln w_n^{kt} \\
& + \frac{1}{2}\alpha_{pp}(\ln p^{kt})^2 + \sum_{n=1}^{N} \alpha_{pn} \ln p^{kt} \ln w_n^{kt} \\
& + \frac{1}{2}\sum_{n=1}^{N}\sum_{n'=1}^{N} \alpha_{nn'} \ln w_n^{kt} \ln w_{n'}^{kt} + v^{kt} - u^{kt}
\end{aligned} \tag{5.5}$$

Following Kumbhakar and Lovell (2000), profit inefficiency may then be expressed as follows:

$$\ln h^{kt}\left(p,w,q,u\right)=-\left[\alpha_p+\alpha_{pp}\ln p^{kt}+\sum_n\alpha_{pn}\ln w_n^{kt}+\eta_{qp}\ln q^{kt}\right]\cdot$$
$$u^{kt}+\frac{1}{2}\alpha_{pp}(u^{kt})^2$$

(5.6)

Symmetry is imposed on the profit function in (5.5) by $\alpha_{n'n}=\alpha_{nn'}$, and linear homogeneity of degree 0 in prices, $(pe^{-u},w)$, is imposed by the following parameter restrictions, $\sum_n\alpha_p+\alpha_n=1$, $\sum_n\alpha_{pn}+\alpha_{pp}=0$, $\sum_{n'}\alpha_{nn'}+\alpha_{pn}=0,\forall n$, and $\sum_n\eta_{qn}+\eta_{qp}=0$.

As previously notified, the underlying production technology is assumed to be homogenous of degree $r$ in inputs, $x$. Therefore, the profit function must also satisfy the following parameter restrictions, $\alpha_{pp}=\alpha_{pn}=\eta_{qp}=0,\forall n$ (see Kumbhakar and Lovell, 2000). This means that the expression in (5.6) collapses to:

$$\ln h(u)^{kt}=-\alpha_p\cdot u^{kt}\text{ with }\alpha_p\geq 1$$

which can be compared with the expression in (5.3).

Assuming that the firms are producing the market product by using the quasi-fixed input factors capital ($K$) and labor ($L$),[2] the variable input factors electricity ($E$) and fossil fuel ($F$), and inserting all the necessary parameter restrictions into Equation (5.5) give the following econometric expression:[3]

$$\ln\left(\frac{\pi^{kt}}{p^{kt}}\right)=\alpha_0+\gamma_K\ln K^{kt}+\gamma_L\ln L^{kt}+\alpha_E\ln(\frac{w_E^{kt}}{p^{kt}})+\alpha_F\ln(\frac{w_F^{kt}}{p^{kt}})$$
$$+\frac{1}{2}\gamma_{KK}\left(\ln K^{kt}\right)^2+\gamma_{KL}\ln K^{kt}\ln L^{kt}+\eta_{KE}\ln K^{kt}\ln(\frac{w_E^{kt}}{w_F^{kt}})$$
$$+\frac{1}{2}\gamma_{LL}\left(\ln L^{kt}\right)^2+\eta_{LE}\ln L^{kt}\ln(\frac{w_E^{kt}}{w_F^{kt}})$$
$$+\frac{1}{2}\alpha_{EE}\left(\ln(\frac{w_E^{kt}}{w_F^{kt}})\right)^2$$
$$+\alpha_T T+v^{kt}-u^{kt}$$

(5.7)

where $1-\alpha_E-\alpha_F=\alpha_p$, $\alpha_{EE}=-\alpha_{EF}=\alpha_{FF}$, and $-\eta_{KE}=\eta_{KF}$.

The profit function in Equation (5.7) is convex and continuous in prices, nondecreasing in $p$ and nonincreasing in $w$, and concave and continuous in fixed input factors (see, e.g., Bergman, 1997). Finally, $T$ is Hicks neutral technological development.

### 5.1.4 Profit efficiency and the $CO_2$ tax

The main purpose of this paper is to test whether the $CO_2$ tax regime in Sweden has had any effects on firms' profit technical efficiency. Therefore, the expression in Equation (5.2) also needs to be explicitly specified, meaning that relevant explanatory $z_{kt}$ variables need to be identified. Here, we follow Managi et al. (2005) and Lanoie et al. (2008) and allow for dynamic effects of environmental policy on firm performance. Specifically, the empirical profit efficiency model reads as follows:

$$-u^{kt} = \delta_0 + \delta_1 tax(CO_2)^{kt} + \delta_2 tax(CO_2)^{kt}_{lag} + \delta_3 Capin^{kt} + \delta_4 Fuelin^{kt}$$
$$+ \sum_{s=1}^{S-1} \delta_5 D^s_{size} + g(t) + v^{kt} \quad (5.8)$$

which, following Battese and Coelli (1995), is estimated simultaneously with Equation (5.7).[4] The explanatory variables of particular interest are $tax(CO_2)^{kt}$, which captures the contemporaneous (static) effect of the $CO_2$ tax on profit efficiency, and $tax(CO_2)^k_{lag}$, which captures the dynamic effects. The latter variable is constructed as a moving average of three lags,

$$tax(CO_2)^k_{lag} = (tax(CO_2)^{kt-1} + tax(CO_2)^{kt-2} + tax(CO_2)^{kt-3})/3$$

This construction of a moving lag variable is chosen to reduce the number of parameters in the ML estimation. To account for firms being of different types, which possibly could have an effect on profit efficiency, variables that represent firm characteristics are included: capital intensity, $Capin^{kt} = K^{kt}/L^{kt}$, and fossil fuel intensity, $Fuelin^{kt} = F^{kt}/L^{kt}$.[5] Furthermore, efficiency may vary due to size-specific profit frontiers. Therefore, size dummies, $D^s_{size}$, are included. Firms are divided into size quartiles, $s = 1,...,4$, based on number of employees. All firms within a certain size class are compared with the profit frontier of that class, and deviation from the frontier is due to heterogeneity in technology and/or management. Finally, to account for time effects on profit efficiency, e.g., booms, recessions, and other time-specific events that are not related to Hicks neutral technological development in the profit function, we add $g(t) = \delta_t t + \delta_{t2} t^2$.[6]

The parameters to be estimated in the inefficiency equation are $\delta_0, \delta_1, \delta_2, \delta_3, \delta_4, \delta_5, \delta_t$, and $\delta_{t2}$. Particular focus is then on the significance of the estimated parameters of contemporaneous and dynamic effects of $CO_2$ taxation, $\hat{\delta}_1$ and $\hat{\delta}_2$, respectively, since they tell us about the validity of the Porter hypothesis. Based on the hypothesis suggesting that there are positive dynamic effects of environmental regulation on profits, the $\hat{\delta}_2$ estimate is expected to take a positive sign. On the other hand, the $\hat{\delta}_1$ estimate can be viewed as capturing static effects of $CO_2$ taxation. Porter and van der Linde (1995) see the traditional neoclassical view on environmental regulation as being static and too narrow. Therefore, it seems natural not to exclude the possibility of a negative sign for $\hat{\delta}_1$.

In the presence of both technical and allocative inefficiency, the single-equation method adopted in this paper has a shortcoming; it is not possible to separate the effect of technical inefficiency and the effect of allocative inefficiency on firm profits. To separate these effects, a system approach is required (see, e.g., the shadow price approach in Kumbhakar and Lovell, 2000).

### 5.1.5   Data

The data contains information from all firms in the manufacturing sectors in Sweden (SNI 10–37). The data set is a firm-level balanced panel covering the years 1990 to 2004.[7] Eleven manufacturing sectors and one extraction sector are included in the empirical application: Food, Textile, Wood, Pulp/Paper, Printing, Chemical, Rubber/Plastic, Mineral/Stone, Iron/Steel, Machine/Electro, Motor vehicles, and Mining. The data contains firms with more than five employees and includes data on output (sales) and input data on quantities and values of labor, electricity and fuels,[8] and gross investment. Capital stocks are calculated using gross investment data and the perpetual inventory method together with the assumption that capital stocks are in steady state in 1990.[9] The data also contains detailed information on emissions of $CO_2$ and total payment of $CO_2$ tax for each firm. We do not have data on, or can reliably construct, marginal taxes that each firm faces. Therefore, we construct a variable for "effective" $CO_2$ tax that varies across firms and sectors and over time, measured as the average tax rate paid per kilo of $CO_2$ emitted. This means that we assume the firms react the same to a small tax increase as to a large tax increase, which is conflicting with economic theory and evidence. Unfortunately, this is the best we can do with the data we have. However, looking at the tax paid and emissions, we see that the relationship is linear or close to linear in most sectors, so our approach may not be misrepresentative.

Output price indices[10] are sector specific, and firm-specific input prices can be calculated from the costs and quantities for electricity and fuels. We assume the firms are operating in a competitive environment and that output and input prices are exogenous to the firm.

Descriptive statistics for the different industry sectors are given in Table 5.1 and Figure 5.1.[11] As mentioned above, the $CO_2$ tax varies considerably across sectors, ranging from about 0.04 SEK/kg in the Wood product sector to almost 0.15 SEK/kg for Food. These are considerably lower tax rates than the base tax rate for the manufacturing sectors, which is 21 percent of the statutory tax rate of about 1 SEK/kg (at 2004). However, as explained in Chapter 1, manufacturing firms are subject to a range of exemption rules, which is why we see that the actual tax paid is lower than the statutory tax rate.

*Table 5.1* Descriptive statistics. Mean values 1990–2004 (base = 1990)

| Sector | | | | | | | | | | |
|---|---|---|---|---|---|---|---|---|---|---|
| Variable | Mining | Food | Textile | Wood | Pulp/Paper | Printing | Chemical | Rubber/ Plastic | Mineral/ Stone | Steel/ Iron | Machine/ Electro | Motor vehicles |
| Capital stock (TSEK) | 524777 (1365816) | 259549 (509303) | 97186 (181651) | 88450 (157760) | 775387 (1511305) | 63998 (102548) | 631622 (1717444) | 113645 (186114) | 108487 (178253) | 191806 (479269) | 238416 (752930) | 581917 (2155773) |
| Employees (number of) | 275 (472) | 208 (227) | 148 (120) | 115 (138) | 325 (308) | 142 (269) | 214 (260) | 140 (123) | 129 (122) | 190 (326) | 228 (319) | 466 (1062) |
| Price electricity (SEK/kWh) | 0.292 (0.126) | 0.279 (0.080) | 0.293 (0.093) | 0.296 (0.096) | 0.240 (0.087) | 0.314 (0.096) | 0.259 (0.105) | 0.282 (0.074) | 0.306 (0.096) | 0.292 (0.086) | 0.314 (0.093) | 0.303 (0.091) |
| Price fossil fuel (SEK/kWh) | 0.282 (0.112) | 0.286 (0.456) | 0.341 (0.179) | 0.359 (0.175) | 0.235 (0.150) | 0.494 (0.205) | 0.272 (0.152) | 0.369 (0.165) | 0.235 (0.115) | 0.314 (0.146) | 0.395 (0.161) | 0.137 (0.134) |
| $CO_2$ tax (SEK/Kg) | 0.074 (0.068) | 0.145 (0.063) | 0.127 (0.078) | 0.041 (0.064) | 0.125 (0.070) | 0.058 (0.076) | 0.123 (0.079) | 0.111 (0.081) | 0.134 (0.065) | 0.137 (0.069) | 0.108 (0.078) | 0.137 (0.065) |
| NOBS | 193 | 2037 | 399 | 1800 | 1285 | 945 | 974 | 917 | 1042 | 2753 | 3649 | 1098 |

Note: Standard deviation in parenthesis.

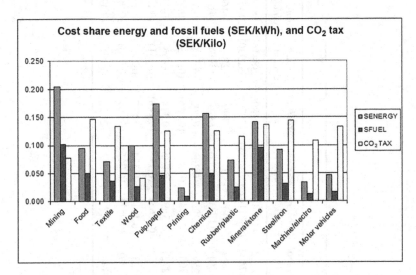

*Figure 5.1* Cost share for energy and fossil fuels, and CO$_2$ tax rate (SEK/kWh)

The system of tax refund is complicated and may appear opaque to a non-expert. This observation is strengthened by the fact that it is difficult to discern from Figure 5.1 any particular pattern or relationship between the cost shares of energy and/or fuels and the actual CO$_2$ tax paid by firms. High use of CO$_2$-emitting inputs does not necessarily mean high CO$_2$ tax/kg, or vice versa.

### 5.1.6   Results: profit efficiency and the CO$_2$ tax

Estimations were performed for all 13 individual sectors, and two different econometric specifications of the profit function were explored. The profit function and the (in)efficiency part of the error term were estimated simultaneously using maximum likelihood techniques (see Appendix 5 for the likelihood function). Table 5.2 contains summarized results (details in Lundgren and Marklund, 2016). The results we select to present here are the ones with profit function parameters satisfying the desired homogeneity property ($r > 0$) and when SIGMA and GAMMA are statistically significant (i.e., there is evidence of inefficiency).[12] Those estimations that do not satisfy these properties cast doubt on the estimated efficiency scores.

Our first observation is that there is inefficiency in all the sectors. This is apparent since the GAMMA and SIGMA columns display statistically significant estimates (which means we are observing inefficiencies). The

*Table 5.2* Summarized results for the Translog specification

| Sector | Static effect of CO$_2$ tax $\delta_1$ | Dynamic effect of CO$_2$ tax $\delta_2$ | Profit efficiency score | GAMMA $\gamma = \sigma_u^2/\sigma_\varepsilon^2$ | SIGMA $\sigma_{\varepsilon=v-u}^2$ | Energy intensive | Number of obs. |
|---|---|---|---|---|---|---|---|
| Mining | 1.399 | 5.415** | 0.539 | 0.833*** | 0.150*** | Yes | 141 |
| Food | −0.625 | 1.369** | 0.567 | 0.672*** | 0.338*** | Yes | 1503 |
| Textile | −3.256 | 5.463* | 0.442 | 0.947*** | 0.480*** | No | 269 |
| Pulp/Paper | −0.850** | −0.990** | 0.661 | 0.503*** | 0.126*** | Yes | 951 |
| Printing | 0.051 | 0.377 | 0.572 | 0.588*** | 0.153*** | No | 639 |
| Chemical | 3.337* | −3.889* | 0.760 | 0.445*** | 0.491*** | Yes | 688 |
| Stone/ Mineral | 2.211*** | −1.876*** | 0.569 | 0.887*** | 0.224*** | Yes | 788 |
| Steel/Iron | −0.248 | 0.012 | 0.632 | 0.514*** | 0.353*** | Yes | 1882 |
| Electro | −0.751** | −0.449 | 0.465 | 0.935*** | 0.183*** | No | 737 |

*Significant at 10% level. **Significant at 5% level. ***Significant at 1% level.

average profit efficiency scores range between 0.442 (Textile) and 0.760 (Chemical), which indicates that profit technical inefficiency is substantial. One reasonable explanation is that this outcome, even though we control for size effects and other characteristics, indicates somewhat heterogeneous firms.[13] Furthermore, statistically significant and positive dynamic (Porter) effects are found in Mining, Food, and Textile. In these sectors, the static effect is nonsignificant.[14] Pulp and Paper shows significant negative effects of the CO$_2$ tax, both the static and dynamic case, on profit efficiency. This indicates that the CO$_2$ tax disturbs production in Pulp and Paper immediately, and that the firms are not able to take measures, either immediately or in the longer term, that neutralize the negative effect of taxation. Chemical and Stone/Mineral show a significant positive static effect, while the dynamic effect is negative; the net effect is, however, negative in Stone/Mineral. A positive static effect indicates that these industries quickly relate CO$_2$ taxation to resource inefficiency in production, and that they successfully take measures immediately. However, in the longer term these measures come with costs in terms of deteriorated ability to maintain efficiency in production. In Electro, CO$_2$ taxation has a significant negative static impact on profit efficiency, but there is no longer term impact. Profit efficiency in Printing and Steel/Iron seems unaffected by the CO$_2$ tax.

Other potential effects on profit efficiency, not explicitly reported above,[15] are firm characteristics and a time-trend (possibly nonlinear). Size matters in some sectors; however, the sign of that effect is ambiguous. Capital intensity seems to be negatively related to efficiency in most sectors (Mining and

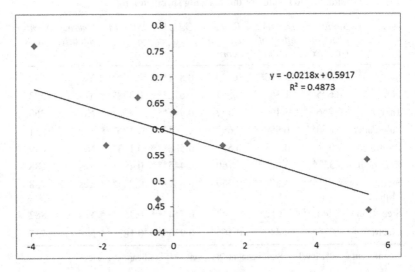

*Figure 5.2* Dynamic effect $\delta_2$ (x-axis) vs. efficiency score (y-axis), sector-level estimates

Textile are exceptions), while the effect of fuel intensity is unclear. Food and Pulp/Paper show an initial negative time-trend in efficiency, but towards the end of the period studied, it turns upward. Other sectors show no clear evidence of time effects.

Is there no detectable pattern in terms of inefficiency and the $CO_2$ tax across sectors? Without having any ambitions other than to illustrate an interesting question, in Figure 5.2 we plot the dynamic effect (x-axis) and the efficiency score (y-axis). An ocular inspection (and a trend line) indicates that efficient firms "suffer" (in terms of efficiency) from the tax, while relatively more inefficient sectors improve their efficiency. Without drawing any stronger conclusions, this suggests that there could be an asymmetric effect of taxation on efficiency; i.e., there could be a dynamic Porter effect for the sectors that are most inefficient. However, whether this is a valid conclusion or not needs to be confirmed by more comprehensive and deeper studies.[16]

### 5.1.7  Conclusions: the $CO_2$ tax and profit efficiency

According to the strong version of the Porter hypothesis, properly crafted environmental regulations have positive dynamic effects on firms' performance in terms of increased productivity and competitiveness. Productivity is determined by the two components, technical efficiency and technological level. In this paper, the main purpose has been to assess empirically the dynamic effects of the Swedish $CO_2$ tax scheme on manufacturing firms' profit efficiency (a constant multiple of technical efficiency), during the period 1990 to 2004. Particularly, we have assessed the effects of $CO_2$ taxation on profit efficiency via effects on firms' use of energy input. The task has been accomplished by using a stochastic frontier approach.

Overall, the result shows that the effect of $CO_2$ taxation on profit efficiency in Swedish industry is not unambiguous. However, on a more general level it seems like the most inefficient sectors become more efficient when they are taxed, and that the most efficient sectors become less efficient. One reasonable explanation in line with the Porter hypothesis is that the increased tax payments make the firms within the inefficient sectors become aware of the inefficiencies and then begin to deal with it. However, the firms within the more efficient sectors do not have this ability to the same extent. To cut the tax costs, they instead invest in innovations to develop more productive and less polluting technologies. When firms begin to use newly developed technologies, there will be learning costs to consider. During the learning period, the firms will operate technically inefficiently below the new technological frontier. That is, innovation-based solutions spurred by taxation cause short-/mid-term costs (in our case two years), which in the analysis appears as increased profit inefficiency. In the defense of the Porter hypothesis, the net effect on productivity may still be positive as technological development can fully offset the decreased profit efficiency. However, this has to be confirmed (or rejected) by future research.

How does our paper relate to previous international literature? Porter and van der Linde (1995) has become one of the most cited articles in the field of research that combines the disciplines of business and environment (Ambec et al., 2013). Both theoretical and empirical studies on various industry sectors have been conducted. However, there are relatively few empirical studies that analyze the impact of what Porter and van der Linde (1995, p. 98) argue to be "properly crafted environmental regulations", i.e., primarily market-based instruments such as pollution taxes and tradable permits (Lanoie et al., 2011). Moreover, Ambec et al. emphasize that previous empirical studies of the Porter hypothesis have not adequately accounted for the dynamic dimension of the hypothesis. This means that environmental regulations are not usually allowed to have lagged impact on productivity and competitiveness and, therefore, it can be questioned whether these studies really test the Porter hypothesis. In this paper, we analyze the effect of a properly crafted environmental instrument ($CO_2$ tax) and allow for lagged effect on profit efficiency (dynamic dimension).

To our knowledge, the only studies that have attempted to measure lagged effects of environmental regulations on firms' productivity over several years are Managi et al. (2005), Lanoie et al. (2008), and Broberg et al. (2013). The results presented in these studies are not unambiguous. Managi et al. found no significant effect of environmental regulations on productivity change and technological development in production of the market goods oil and gas in the Gulf of Mexico (this does not necessarily exclude positive effect on technical efficiency change). Lanoie et al. reported that environmental regulations have positive lagged effects on productivity, i.e., technological development (they assume that there is no technical inefficiency) in manufacturing in Quebec, Canada. They also found that the positive lagged effects are stronger in sectors that are more exposed to international competition.[17] Broberg et al. found indications of environmental regulations leading to losses in the technical efficiency component of productivity in Swedish industry, particularly strong in Pulp and Paper. However, whether the results presented in these studies can be used to judge the Porter hypothesis is questionable in one respect; the measures used as proxies for environmental regulations, e.g., cost of complying with command-and-control types of environmental regulations and investments in pollution control (e.g., end-of-pipe equipment), do not capture properly crafted environmental regulations. According to Porter and van der Linde (1995), command-and-control policies should be seen as a last resort. Broberg et al. use the firms' investments in pollution prevention as a proxy of environmental regulation. However, these investments are not necessarily triggered by market-based policy instruments.

A study that analyzes the impact of a market-based instrument is Brännlund and Lundgren (2010). They report an overall negative impact of $CO_2$ taxation on profits in Swedish energy-intensive industries. However, they only take into account the short-term static effect, and the results cannot be used to judge the Porter hypothesis (Porter and van der Linde, 1995, do not rule out short-term costs due to, e.g., learning effects). Our study complements that of Brännlund and Lundgren. Using a subset of their data, we have broadened the picture of the impact of $CO_2$ taxation and especially its dynamic mid-term effects on efficiency and profits in Swedish manufacturing.

There are several interesting topics of future research in this area. For example, a natural step would be to also allow for allocative inefficiency in production and analyze whether $CO_2$ taxation has impact on this type of efficiency. This would indicate whether taxation has effect on firms' input mix in production, e.g., different types of energy inputs, which is a particularly important research question in support for climate policy. Furthermore, the EU attaches great importance to tradable permits via its emissions trading system (EU ETS). The literature on environmental regulation and its impact on firm performance, in terms of giving incentives to productivity growth, is extensive, but rarely considers tradable permits such as the EU ETS. As data from the first trading period, 2005–2008, is becoming readily available, more applications to the EU ETS are to be expected (one recent example is Jaraite and Di Maria, 2011). Also, simultaneously assessing how environmental policy, such as the $CO_2$ tax, is connected to actual environmental performance of firms and, in turn, its relation to firm profitability, would give a more complete view of how policy and different types of firm performance are linked together.

## 5.2   The $CO_2$ tax, environmental performance, and profits

We now turn to shed light on the role of environmental performance (EP) and its effect on profit efficiency (PE), a study documented entirely in Lundgren and Marklund (2015). The model, data, and frontier/efficiency estimation approach are exactly the same as the profit frontier study presented above, so there is no need to repeat all the details concerning those issues. EP is measured as described in Chapter 2 and applied in Chapter 4 (Brännlund et al., 2014) and describes changes in firm-level $CO_2$ intensity in production. From Chapter 4, we know that EP has improved in all sectors in Swedish manufacturing since the $CO_2$ tax scheme was introduced in 1991; production increased at the same time as emissions decreased in most sectors. The tax contributed significantly to this development.

A positive relationship between EP and PE means there are not only environmental gains to be expected from increasing EP, but also private gains for firms in terms of improved competitiveness, which is in line with the Porter argument. Normally, in the literature (especially in business/management and finance), EP is proxied by third-party ratings provided by consulting firms, and economic performance is usually a financial measure (return on assets, Tobin's q, etc.).[18] Paul and Siegel (2006) note that the massive amount of studies on corporate social responsibility (CSR) ratings and the effects on financial measures is unsatisfactory. They propose that a more relevant question is the relationship between *actual* EP and economic performance, where economic performance entails technological and economic interactions between the production of output and input utilization, recognizing the opportunity costs of various inputs and capital formation. This is what we attempt to do in this study.

The empirical analysis is performed in three stages: (1) a Malmquist-type of quantity index is used to measure EP; (2) variation in EP induced by policy is determined; and (3) the effects of market or voluntary driven changes in EP on PE are evaluated.

The empirical approach lets us investigate the *whole chain*, from the impact of CO$_2$ taxation on firms' EP to the impact of policy-induced and market-driven EP on PE.

The EP index reveals the change of the relationship between firms' good output and bad output, in our case between a marketed output index and the emissions of CO$_2$. Adopting a methodological approach comparable to Hamamoto (2006) and Yang et al. (2012), we isolate variation in predicted EP into CO$_2$ tax–triggered variation and variation due to market-determined factors. Market-driven EP is triggered by factors other than CO$_2$ taxation, such as fossil fuel price and firm characteristics, or by changed preferences for the environment in firms and society, which may include purely strategic reasons (improved EP is simply "good business"). Finally, PE scores are estimated using a stochastic frontier analysis approach, where efficiency is allowed to depend on both types of EP.

### 5.2.1   Environmental performance: the index

As outlined in Chapter 2 and described in Chapter 4 (Equation 4.1), we start from production theory and, based on ratios of Shephard-type output distance functions, derive an index that describes changes in firm $k$'s CO$_2$ intensity in production between period $t - 1$ and $t$; we here denote this index $EP^{k,t}$. Remember that if the index changes for the worse, then $EP^{k,t} < 1$, or improves, then $EP^{k,t} > 1$.

### 5.2.2   Deriving policy-induced variation in EP

To separate variation in EP into CO$_2$ tax–triggered variation and variation due to market driven or voluntarily actions by firms, we embrace a methodological approach similar to Hamamoto (2006) and Yang et al. (2012). We estimate a function that relates the variable of interest (EP) to a policy variable (effective CO$_2$ tax).

It is assumed that EP is determined mainly by the previous period CO$_2$ tax (*taxCO$_2$*) and the price of fossil fuels (*pf*). We control for firm characteristics, the cost share of fossil fuels (*sfuel*), capital intensity (capital stock over total employees, *kapin*), a size effect (*size*), and a nonlinear time-trend (*trend*), that captures technological progress and/or increased environmental awareness/pressure on firms during the period studied. For the general form of this relationship, we write:

$$EP^{k,t} = f\left[taxCO_2^{k,t-1}, pf^{k,t-1}, \mathbf{X}^{k,t-1}\right] \tag{5.9}$$

where $\mathbf{X}^{k,t-1} = [sfuel^{k,t-1}, kapin^{k,t-1}, size^{k,t-1}, trend]$ is a vector of control variables. EP is expected to be increasing in the tax and fossil fuel price.

As described in Chapter 4, a log-linear function for EP is estimated,

$$\ln(EP)^{k,t} = c_k + a_1 \ln(taxCO_2^{k,t-1}) + a_2 \ln(pf^{k,t-1})$$

$$+ a_3 \ln(sfuel^{k,t-1}) + a_4 \ln(kapin^{k,t-1}) + \sum_{size}^{4-1} a_{5size}size^{k,t-1} \quad (5.10)$$

$$+ a_6 trend + a_7(trend)^2 + e^{k,t}$$

where $e^{k,t}$ is an error term.

To isolate the variation in firms' EP due to the $CO_2$ tax, we follow Hamamoto (2006) and Yang et al. (2012), and predicted values are derived as

$$\hat{EP1}^{k,t} = \hat{a}_1(\Delta taxCO_2^{k,t,t-1}) \frac{EP^{k,t}}{taxCO_2^{k,t-1}} \quad (5.11)$$

where $\hat{a}_1$ is the tax elasticity. The remaining variation is calculated as a residual

$$\hat{EP2}^{k,t} = EP^{k,t} - \hat{EP1}^{k,t} \quad (5.12)$$

and constitutes the market-driven or voluntary variation in EP. It stems from firms adjusting to factors other than $CO_2$ taxation, e.g., increased energy prices, or acting strategically as a reaction to changed environmental preferences on markets.[19]

Lundgren and Marklund (2015) use the EP indexes in Brännlund et al. (2014) together with the tax elasticities to compute *EP1* and *EP2*; see these two articles and Chapter 4 for details.

### 5.2.3 Profit efficiency and environmental performance

Using the same frontier model as in Section 5.1.3, we explicitly test the effects of environmental performance on profit efficiency. The inefficiency equation is modeled as:

$$-u^{k,t} = \delta_0 + \delta_1(\hat{EP1})^{k,t-1} + \delta_2(\hat{EP2})^{k,t-1} + \delta_3 kapin^{k,t-1}$$

$$+ \delta_4 fuelin^{k,t-1} + \sum_{s=1}^{S-1} \delta_{5s} size^{k,t-1} + \delta_t trend + v^{k,t}. \quad (5.13)$$

Capital intensity is denoted $kapin^{k,t-1}$ (capital stock over employees), and $fuelin^{k,t-1}$ is fuel intensity (fuel over employees). Size dummies are also included, $size^{k,t-1}$, which are based on number of employees. Also, a trend variable, *trend*, is included. Finally, $v^{k,t}$ is white noise. T-tests are performed on the estimates $\hat{\delta}_1$ and $\hat{\delta}_2$ in order to evaluate the effect that EP (and indirectly the tax) has on profit efficiency.

### 5.2.4    Results: environmental performance and profit efficiency

In Table 5.3, the main results are summarized. Results reveal that all sectors are inefficient. Policy-induced EP does have a significant and positive effect (the so-called Porter effect) on profit efficiency in Chemical and the aggregate Non-energy intensive firms. Profit efficiency in the industry as a whole responds positively and significantly to what we label voluntary EP. Results from different subsectors, and the aggregate Energy intensive firms, confirm this general result with a few exceptions; Pulp/Paper and Rubber/Plastic show a significant negative relationship between profits and EP, while a few other sectors show no link at all. The policy-induced EP shares vary between sectors with the highest shares recorded in Wood and Pulp/Paper.

Results suggest that voluntary or market-driven EP in general seems to motivate firms to be more profit efficient, while policy-induced EP is not a relevant determinant of profit efficiency. Again, in line with Lundgren and Marklund (2016), which is presented in the first part of this chapter, the general evidence speaks against the Porter hypothesis, since policy is statistically insignificant or has a neutral effect on profit efficiency.

*Table 5.3* Impact of EP on profit efficiency

| Sector | EP1 | EP2 | PE | EP1 share |
|---|---|---|---|---|
| Manufacturing | 0.100 | 0.077*** | 0.786 | 0.046 |
| Mining | −1.147 | −0.060 | 0.573 | 0.035 |
| Food | −0.256 | 0.122** | 0.665 | 0.010 |
| Textile | 0.217 | 0.532** | 0.696 | 0.028 |
| Wood | 0.896 | 0.994 | 0.747 | 0.124 |
| Pulp/Paper | −0.085** | −0.069*** | 0.571 | 0.176 |
| Printing | −6.368 | 0.092 | 0.602 | 0.001 |
| Chemical | 0.139* | 0.128** | 0.469 | 0.114 |
| Rubber/Plastic | 0.039 | −0.073** | 0.737 | 0.041 |
| Stone/Mineral | −0.025 | 0.097*** | 0.351 | 0.052 |
| Steel/Iron | 0.003 | 0.039 | 0.416 | 0.011 |
| Machinery | −0.404 | 0.097*** | 0.362 | 0.000 |
| Electro | −23.21 | 0.184 | 0.787 | 0.000 |
| Motor vehicles | 0.036 | 0.067** | 0.495 | 0.054 |
| Energy int. | 0.090 | 0.074* | 0.788 | 0.067 |
| Non-energy int. | 0.209* | 0.138*** | 0.685 | 0.021 |

Source: Lundgren and Marklund, 2015

* Significant at 10% level. **Significant at 5% level. ***Significant at 1% level.

### 5.2.5 Conclusions: environmental performance and profit efficiency

The main conclusion is that policy-induced EP is not an important determinant of profit efficiency – it has a neutral effect in most cases – but voluntary or market-driven EP seems to drive firms to be more profit efficient. It should be noted, however, that policy-induced variation in EP constitutes a relatively small part of total variation in EP (about 5% on average).

The results presented here are in line with the various empirical studies that show a positive connection between financial performance measures and environmental performance in terms of third-party, subjective ranking measures (see, e.g., review by Orlitzky and Swanson, 2008). However, our evidence is generated differently, using a methodology where the performance measures are derived from actual firm behavior, and we take into account firm technology by explicitly allowing for interactions and trade-offs between different uses of energy inputs and the production of outputs.

Results suggest that environmental policy (via EP) is not an important driver of firm performance in Swedish industry. This result disagrees with Hamamoto (2006), who finds that policy (via R&D) is promoting performance in terms of total factor productivity in Japanese industry. However, our results are generally in line with many studies on the so-called Porter effect that find no convincing evidence of a "win-win" outcome of environmental policy (see, e.g., Brännlund and Lundgren, 2009). Since policy-induced EP seems to have a neutral effect on profit efficiency, it indicates that measures taken to improve EP as a result of an increase in regulatory pressure are neither promoting nor impeding PE. The neutrality of policy on profits is good news for both policy makers and firms; the environment can be improved via a tax scheme policy without imposing additional inefficiencies on the firm.

## 5.3 Notes

1 To test whether there is any technical inefficiency at all, a significance test of the $\gamma$ estimate can be run (see Coelli, 1996).
2 It is often appropriate to apply a short-run framework when estimating profit functions, modeling at least one input as quasi-fixed. Then, the most natural choice is the capital stock. Furthermore, as we aim at assessing the effects of CO$_2$ taxation on energy efficiency use in production, we also model labor as a quasi-fixed factor. It may seem controversial to regard the number of employees as exogenously given in the short run. However, this is not that far from the truth concerning the circumstances in Sweden. By the Swedish Employment Protection Act (Lagen om AnställningsSkydd, LAS 11§), the term of notice is one to six months depending on time of employment. Furthermore, as a complement to LAS, nearly all industrial firms have collective agreement, which is an agreement between employers' and employees' organizations. Not unusual,

the collective agreement is additionally to the benefit of the employees. Hence, the term of notice can, in certain cases, exceed six months in practice. In this respect, both capital and labor (measured as number of employees) are sluggish compared to energy input.

3  Due to limited data, we have not been able to include biofuel as input in production. These inputs are becoming more and more important, especially in certain industries. However, most of the development likely occurred in the last decade, that is, after the last year of our study.

4  See Appendix 5 for specification of log likelihood equation.

5  Elaborating with tax interaction terms did not provide any significant additional information to, or change, our main results.

6  As pointed out in Ambec et al. (2013), the Porter hypothesis argues that tougher environmental regulation leads to investment in R&D, which in turn leads to innovation and productivity increases. This would motivate the inclusion of investment in R&D as a regressor in the inefficiency equation. This means that, since we intend to analyze the effect of CO$_2$ taxation on firms' profit efficiency, it would be appropriate to add information on investments aiming at reducing CO$_2$ emissions. However, we lack the appropriate data for this exercise, and this problem cannot be addressed within the framework of this study. As is stated in Broberg et al. (2013), data on environmental protection investments collected by Statistics Sweden do not systematically cover these types of investments.

7  This is a subset of the unbalanced panel used in Brännlund and Lundgren (2010).

8  Note that 70–80 percent on average of the fossil fuels is oil of some sort. The rest is natural gas and to some small extent coal. We preferred aggregation like this because it simplifies the econometric estimations. It is possible to separate the different fossil fuels and identify substitution, but often we got nonsensible results (probably because oil is dominating).

9  The depreciation rate 0.087 is taken from King and Fullerton (1984) and Bergman (1996), who attempt to estimate industry averages for Sweden. We have gross investment data, so the problem when creating capital stocks is to assign a starting value ($K_0$). We simply do this by assuming that the investment rate in 1990 equals the depreciation of capital that year for all firms, which admittedly is a bold assumption. By this procedure, we are able to "back out" the capital stock for that year. The estimated initial values of capital in 1990 are not crucial for the results, as it is the gross investment that governs the movement of the capital stock. Implicitly, we are assuming there is some relationship between the size of the stock and its flow (gross investments) in 1990. Other ways of assigning initial values for capital stocks, e.g. by using aggregate stocks and weighting with sales to achieve firm stocks, did not alter the results.

10  Collected from Statistics Sweden; see producer price index section at the website www.scb.se.

11  For those readers further interested in data issues, please consult Brännlund and Lundgren (2009, 2010) where the same data source is used.

12  Heterogeneity, especially in some sectors, may cause great variation in efficiency scores. We therefore try to do the sectoral aggregations in a way that this heterogeneity is minimized.

13  Given that firms produce exactly the same marketed product, differences in efficiency scores between firms will then be due to both technical efficiency (firms produce with more or less productive technologies in each of the firm size categories) and management efficiency (the management of a given technology).

14 The dynamic effects are restricted to be constant across the different periods. We tried to relax this restriction by interacting the dynamic effect with time in different ways, but no model specification produced converging estimations.

15 See estimation details in Lundgren and Marklund (2016).

16 In Figure 5.2, the Textile sector is situated the most southeast (the most inefficient) and the Chemical sector to the far northwest (most efficient).

17 Lanoie et al. (2008, p. 123) measure international competition as exports + imports / total shipments. They found that the manufacturing sectors in Quebec, Canada, most exposed to international competition are Leather, Paper and allied products, Primary metals, Machinery, Transportation equipment, Electrical and electronic products, and Chemicals.

18 A review of empirical studies on corporate social responsibility (CSR) and its impact on financial performance is provided in Orlitzky and Swanson (2008). See also Lundgren (2011) for a review of the literature and a general theory of the socially responsible firm and the potential motivations for voluntary responsible behavior.

19 See Orlitzky et al. (2011) for a discussion on strategic or profit-maximizing green behavior.

20 Following Battese and Coelli (1993), we choose to drop the logarithmic prefix to simplify the presentation of the likelihood function and its partial derivatives.

## 5.4 References

Ambec, S., M.A. Cohen, S. Elgie, P. Lanoie, 2013. The Porter Hypothesis at 20: Can Environmental Regulation Enhance Innovation and Competitiveness? *Review of Environmental Economics and Policy* 7(1): 2–22.

Battese, G.E., T.J. Coelli, 1993. A Stochastic Frontier Production Function Incorporating a Model for Technical Inefficiency Effects. Working Papers in Econometrics and Applied Statistics, No 69, Department of Econometrics, University of New England, Armidale.

Battese, G.E., T.J. Coelli, 1995. A Model for Technical Inefficiency Effects in a Stochastic Frontier Production Function for Panel Data. *Empirical Economics* 20(2): 325–332.

Bergman, M., 1996. Estimating Investment Adjustment Costs and Capital Rates from the Production Function. Umeå Economic Studies 406, Umeå University, Sweden.

Bergman, M., 1997. The Restricted Profit Function and the Application of the Generalized Leontief and the Translog Functional Forms. *International Journal of Production Economics* 49(3): 249–254.

Brännlund, R., T. Lundgren, 2009. Environmental Policy without Costs? A Review of the Porter Hypothesis. *International Review of Environmental and Resource Economics* 3(2): 75–117.

Brännlund, R., T. Lundgren, 2010. Environmental Policy and Profitability – Evidence from Swedish Industry. *Environmental Economics and Policy Studies* 12(1–2): 59–78.

Brännlund, R., T. Lundgren, P-O. Marklund, 2014. Carbon Intensity in Production and the Effects of Climate Policy – Evidence from Swedish Industry. *Energy Policy* 61: 844–857.

Broberg, T., P-O. Marklund, E. Samakovlis, H. Hammar, 2013. Testing the Porter Hypothesis: The Effects of Environmental Investments on Efficiency in Swedish Industry. *Journal of Productivity Analysis* 40: 43–56.

Coelli, T.J., 1996. A Guide to FRONTIER Version 4.1: A Computer Program for Frontier Production Function Estimation, CEPA Working Paper No 7/96, Department of Econometric, University of New England, Armidale, Australia.

Hamamoto, M., 2006. Environmental Regulation and the Productivity of Japanese Manufacturing Industries. *Resource and Energy Economics* 28: 299–312.

Jaffe, A.B., K. Palmer, 1997. Environmental Regulation and Innovation: A Panel Data Study. *Review of Economics and Statistics* 79(4): 610–619.

Jaraite, J., C. Di Maria, 2011. Efficiency, Productivity, and Environmental Policy: A Case Study of Power Generation in the EU, CERE Working Paper 2011–3 (www.cere.se).

King, M.A., D. Fullerton, 1984. *The Taxation of Income from Capital*. The University of Chicago Press, Chicago and London.

Kumbhakar, S.C., 2001. Estimation of Profit Functions when Profit is Not Maximum. *American Journal of Agricultural Economics* 83(1): 1–19.

Kumbhakar, S.C., C.A.K. Lovell, 2000. *Stochastic Frontier Analysis*. Cambridge University Press, Cambridge.

Lanoie, P., J. Laurent-Lucchetti, N. Johnstone, S. Ambec, 2011. Environmental Policy, Innovation and Performance: New Insights on the Porter Hypothesis. *Journal of Economics and Management Strategy* 20(3): 803–842.

Lanoie, P., M. Patry, R. Lajeunesse, 2008. Environmental Regulation and Productivity: Testing the Porter Hypothesis. *Journal of Productivity Analysis* 30(2): 121–128.

Lundgren, T., 2011. A Micro-Economic Model of Corporate Social Responsibility. *Metroeconomica* 62(1): 69–95.

Lundgren, T., P-O. Marklund, 2015. Climate Policy, Environmental Performance, and Profits. *Journal of Productivity Analysis* 44(3): 225–235.

Lundgren, T., P-O. Marklund, 2016. An Analysis of the Swedish CO2 Tax and Its Impact on Firm Performance. WP 2016: 1, Centre for Environmental and Resource Economics (www.cere.se/en).

Managi, S., J.J. Opaluch, Di Jin, T.A. Grigalunas, 2005. Environmental Regulations and Technological Change in the Offshore Oil and Gas Industry. *Land Economics* 81(2): 303–319.

Orlitzky, M., S. Siegel, D. Waldman, 2011. Strategic Corporate Social Responsibility and Environmental Sustainability. *Business and Society* 50(1): 6–27.

Orlitzky, M., D. Swanson, 2008. *Toward Integrative Corporate Citizenship: Research Advances in Corporate Social Performance*. Palgrave MacMillan, London.

Paul, C., D. Siegel, eds, 2006. Special Issue on Corporate Social Responsibility (CSR) and Economic Performance. *Journal of Productivity Analysis* 26(3): 207–287.

Porter, M.E., 1991. Americas Green Strategy. *Scientific American* 264: 168.

Porter, M.E., C. van der Linde, 1995. Toward a New Conception of the Environment-Competitiveness Relationship. *Journal of Economic Perspectives* 9(4): 97–118.

Shadbegian, R.J., W.B. Gray, 2006. Assessing Multi-Dimensional Performance: Environmental and Economic Outcomes. *Journal of Productivity Analysis* 26(3): 213–234.

van der Vlist, A.J., C. Withhagen, H. Folmer, 2007. Technical Efficiency under Alternative Environmental Regulatory Regimes: The Case of Dutch Horticulture. *Ecological Economics* 63(1): 165–173.

Yang, C-H., Y-H. Tseng, C-P. Chen, 2012. Environmental Regulations, Induced R&D, and Productivity: Evidence from Taiwan's Manufacturing Industries. *Resource and Energy Economics* 34(4): 514–532.

## 5.5 Appendix 5

Based on the reparameterization of the model, replacing $\sigma_\nu^2$ and $\sigma_u^2$ with $\sigma^2 = \sigma_\nu^2 + \sigma_u^2$ and $\gamma = \sigma_u^2 / \sigma^2$, Battese and Coelli (1993) present the log-likelihood function and its partial derivatives for the stochastic production frontier model. Here we reproduce this function, in a profit function setting, by starting with the assumption that the inefficiency stochastic profit model is expressed by:[20]

$$\pi^{kt} = W^{kt}\alpha + \nu^{kt} - u^{kt}$$
$$u^{kt} = z^{kt}\delta + \upsilon^{kt} \tag{A5.1}$$

where (A5.1) is the profit function. Furthermore, $W^{kt}$ is a vector of output and input prices, and quasi-fixed inputs. Then, given that the number of observations for firm $k$ are $T^k, 1 \leq T^k \leq T$, and $\pi^k \equiv (\pi^{k1}, \pi^{k2}, ..., \pi^{kT_k})'$ is the vector of firm $k$'s $T^k$ profit values in (A5.1), the logarithm of the likelihood function is expressed by (Note that $\pi$ on the left-hand side and $\pi^{kt}$ on the right-hand side denote profit, and $\pi^p$ denotes the mathematical constant pi, 3.14):

$$L(\theta; \pi) = -\frac{1}{2}\left(\sum_{k=1}^{K} T^k\right)\left\{\ln 2\pi^p + \ln \sigma^2\right\}$$

$$-\frac{1}{2}\sum_{k=1}^{K}\sum_{t=1}^{T^k}\left\{(\pi^{kt} - W^{kt}\alpha + z^{kt}\delta)^2 / \sigma^2\right\} \tag{A5.2}$$

$$-\sum_{k=1}^{K}\sum_{t=1}^{T^k}\left\{\ln \Phi(d^{kt}) - \ln \Phi(d^{*,kt})\right\}$$

where $\Phi(\cdot)$ denotes the cumulative distribution function for the standard normal random variable. Furthermore, $\theta = (\alpha', \delta', \sigma^2, \gamma)', d^{kt} = z^{kt}\delta / (\gamma\sigma^2)^{1/2}$, $d^{*,kt} = \mu^{*,kt}/\sigma^*, \mu^{*,kt} = (1-\gamma)z^{kt}\delta - \gamma(\pi^{kt} - W^{kt}\alpha), \sigma^* = \left[\gamma(1-\gamma)\sigma^2\right]^{1/2}$.

The partial derivatives of the likelihood function in (A5.2), with respect to $\alpha, \delta, \sigma^2$ and $\gamma$ are given by ($\phi(\cdot)$ denoting the probability density function for the standard normal random variable):

$$\frac{\partial L^*}{\partial \alpha} = \sum_{k=1}^{K}\sum_{t=1}^{T^k}\left\{\frac{(\pi^{kt} - W^{kt}\alpha + z^{kt}\delta)}{\sigma^2} + \frac{\phi(d^{*,kt})}{\Phi(d^{*,kt})}\cdot\frac{\gamma}{\sigma_u^*}\right\}\cdot W'^{kt},$$

$$\frac{\partial L^*}{\partial \delta} = -\sum_{k=1}^{K}\sum_{t=1}^{T^k}\left\{\frac{(\pi^{kt} - W^{kt}\alpha + z^{kt}\delta)}{\sigma^2} + \left[\frac{\varphi(d^{kt})}{\Phi(d^{kt})}\cdot\frac{1}{(\gamma\sigma^2)^{1/2}} - \frac{\varphi(d^{*,kt})}{\Phi(d^{*,kt})}\cdot\frac{(1-\gamma)}{\sigma_u^*}\right]\right\}\cdot z'^{kt},$$

$$\frac{\partial L^*}{\partial \sigma^2} = -\frac{1}{2}\left(\frac{1}{\sigma^2}\right) \cdot \left[ \begin{array}{l} \left(\displaystyle\sum_{k=1}^{K} T^k\right) - \displaystyle\sum_{k=1}^{K}\sum_{t=1}^{T^k}\left[\frac{\varphi(d^{kt})}{\Phi(d^{kt})} \cdot d^{kt} - \frac{\varphi(d^{*,kt})}{\Phi(d^{*,kt})} \cdot d^{*,kt}\right] \\ -\displaystyle\sum_{k=1}^{K}\sum_{t=1}^{T^k}\frac{(\pi^{kt} - W^{kt}\alpha + z^{kt}\delta)}{\sigma^2} \end{array} \right],$$

$$\frac{\partial L^*}{\partial \gamma} = \sum_{k=1}^{K}\sum_{t=1}^{T^k}\left\{ \frac{\phi(d^{kt})}{\Phi(d^{kt})} \cdot \frac{d^{kt}}{2\gamma} + \frac{\phi(d^{*,kt})}{\Phi(d^{*,kt})}\left[ \begin{array}{l} \dfrac{(\pi^{kt} - W^{kt}\alpha + z^{kt}\delta)}{\sigma_u^*} \\ +\dfrac{d^{*,kt}(1-2\gamma)}{2\gamma(1-\gamma)\sigma^{2*}} \end{array} \right] \right\}.$$

# 6 Regulation and unintended consequences

## Which bad is worst?

In this chapter, we study the jointness of production of good and bad outputs. Production of a desirable output such as kWh of electricity is often accompanied by the production of an undesirable or bad output such as sulfur dioxide ($SO_2$), or as Baumgärtner et al. (2001, p. 365) stated "the production of wanted goods gives rise to additional unwanted outputs". In addition, the bad outputs are often regulated in the sense that their production is not allowed to exceed a certain level.

Here we analyze what we call unintended consequences of (quantity) regulation of bads.[1] We first prove a theorem using one good and one bad output that explains how quantity regulation may impose bounds on the desirable output. We introduce the notion that a bad output may be limitational and relate it to the notion of null-jointness discussed in Chapter 2.

The second part of the chapter introduces a methodology in the spirit of L. Johansen (1968) that allows us to rank the bad outputs with respect to how strongly each of them restricts the production of the desirable output. We apply our model to Swedish pulp and paper data at the firm level covering the period 1998 to 2008, focusing especially on the year 2008.

## 6.1 Unintended consequences

In this section, we analyze what we call the unintended consequences of regulation of bads where that regulation limits the quantity of bads produced. We consider the simple case in which there is one good and one bad output. Under constant returns to scale, we provide a theorem that characterizes the situation in which quantity regulation of the bad output restricts the production of the intended good output. Our theorem is in the spirit of Shephard's proof of the Law of Diminishing Returns, see Shephard and Färe (1974).[2]

We begin with the axiomatic framework of technology, in which good and bad outputs are jointly produced.[3] In terms of notation, let $y \geq 0$ denote the single desirable output and $b \geq 0$ the only undesirable output. Inputs are denoted by $x = (x_1, \ldots, x_N) \in \Re_+^N$. The technology is modeled by its output correspondence

$$P(x) = \{ (y,b) : x \text{ can produce } (y,b) \}, x \in \Re_+^N.$$

As in Chapter 2, we follow Shephard (1970b) and make the following assumptions on technology $P(x)$.

- $P(0) = 0$, inactivity.
- $P(x)$ is bounded for all $x \in \Re_+^N$, scarcity.
- $P(x') \supseteq P(x)$ when $x' \geq x$, strong disposability of inputs.
- $(y,b) \in P(x)$ and $0 \leq \lambda \leq 1 \Rightarrow (\lambda y, \lambda b) \in P(x)$, weak disposability of outputs.
- $P(x)$ is closed and nonempty.

The axioms itemized above on technology are – with the exception of weak disposability of outputs – consistent with traditional production theory. These are discussed in detail elsewhere, for example, see in Färe and Grosskopf (2004). Here we also assume that $P(x)$ is homogeneous of degree +1 (constant returns to scale).

One of the distinguishing features of production in the presence of good and bad outputs is based on thermodynamics; as Baumgärtner et al. (2001, p. 365) state "the production of wanted goods gives rise to additional unwanted outputs", which states that bad outputs are essential byproducts of the production of good outputs. Shephard and Färe (1974) model this condition by introducing what they call null-joint production, i.e.,

If $(y,b) \in P(x)$, and $b = 0$ then $y = 0$.

This says that if production is null-joint, in order to produce good output, some bad output or byproduct will also be produced – no fire without smoke.

A simple example that satisfies our axioms is

$$P(x) = \{ (y,b) : y + (b - 1/2y) \leq x \quad \text{if } (b - 1/2y) \geq 0 \\ 0 \qquad\qquad\qquad \text{otherwise} \}.$$

Figure 6.1 illustrates.

This output set has input $x = 1$, and the boundary of the set is the triangle 0a1. Note that this satisfies null-jointness, since if $b = 0$ then for $(y,b)$ to be feasible, it must be true that $y = 0$.

We will eventually show that bounds on bad production limit good output production as well. To model this idea we introduce the following definition:

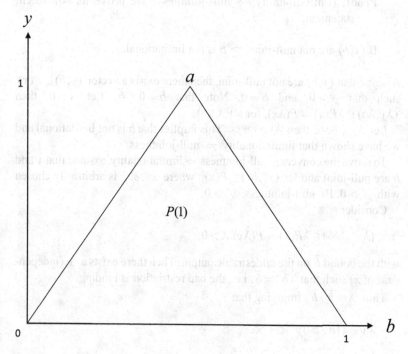

*Figure 6.1* An output set with weakly disposable and null-joint outputs

The bad output is limitational[4] if for all $\bar{b} \geq 0$ :

$$\sup_{x \in \Re_+^N} \{ y : (y,b) \in P(x), b \leq \bar{b} \} < +\infty.$$

In words, if the bad output may not exceed $\bar{b}$, the "largest" feasible production of good output is finite with any level of input consistent with $x \in \Re_+^N$. Thus limitationality models the question we are interested in: Do regulations limiting the production of bad outputs affect production of the good output? If bads are limitational, the answer is yes. The following theorem characterizes the limitationality of $b$.

**Theorem:** Let $P(x)$ be homogeneous of degree $+1$ and satisfy the Shephard axioms above, then $b$ is limitational if and only if $y$ and $b$ are null-joint.

**Proof:** (limitationality $\Rightarrow$ null-jointness) We prove its equivalent statement:

If $(y,b)$ are not null-joint $\Rightarrow b$ is not limitational.

Assume that $(y,b)$ are not null-joint, then there exists a vector $(y,b) \in P(x)$ such that $y > 0$ and $b = 0$. Note that $b = 0 \leq \bar{b}$. Let $\lambda > 0$, then $(\lambda y, \lambda b) \in \lambda P(x) = P(\lambda x)$, for all $\lambda > 0$.

Let $\lambda \to +\infty$, then $\lambda y \to +\infty$. This implies that $b$ is not limitational and we have shown that limitationality $\Rightarrow$ null-jointness.

To prove the converse, null-jointness $\Rightarrow$ limitationality, assume that $y$ and $b$ are null-joint and let $(y^o, b^o) \in P(x)$, where $x \in \Re_+^N$ is arbitrarily chosen with $y^o > 0$. By null-jointness, $b^o > 0$.

Consider

$$(\lambda y^o, \lambda b^o) \in \lambda P(x) = P(\lambda x), \lambda > 0,$$

with the bound $\bar{b}$ on the undesirable output. Then there exists a $\hat{\lambda}$ (independent of $x$) such that $\hat{\lambda} b^o = \bar{b}$, i.e., the bad restriction is binding.

Thus $\hat{\lambda} = \bar{b} / b^o$ implying that

$$\hat{\lambda} y^o = (\bar{b} / b^o) y^o < +\infty.$$

Thus $b$ is limitational.

Q.E.D.

This theorem tells us that under constant returns to scale[5] (as in long run equilibrium) if the undesirable output $b$ is quantity-regulated, i.e., $b \leq \bar{b}$, then the desirable output is bounded given that the two outputs are null-joint, even if inputs are allowed to increase without limit.

This undesirable result can be at least partially circumvented by introducing technical change, so that "more good can be produced with the given bad". In terms of our example, we would introduce a technical change factor, say $h(t)$, such that

$$P(x,t) = \{(y,b) : y + (b - h(t)y) \leq x \quad \text{if } (b - h(t)y) \geq 0$$
$$0 \qquad\qquad\qquad \text{otherwise}\},$$

with $h(t)$ decreasing over time. This might be called "green" technical change.

## 6.2   Which bad is worst?

In this section, we assume there are $b_j$, $j = 1 \ldots J$, bad outputs and we rank them with respect to how they restrict the production of the single good output.

Our model is in the spirit of L. Johansen's (1968) capacity model but applied to good and bad outputs. That is, we measure how much more good output could be produced if $b_j$ for each $j$ is not regulated. This output level is compared to that good output level that would be achieved when all bad outputs are regulated (at their observed values).

We use a DEA model to estimate the different output levels. In Section 6.3, we apply our model to a Swedish data set of the pulp and paper industry at the firm level.

Assume that there are $k = 1 \ldots K$ observations (firms) using $x^k = (x_{k1}, \ldots, x_{kN}) \in \Re_+^N$ to produce a single desirable or good output $y$ and $b^k = (b_{k1}, \ldots, b_{kJ}) \in \Re_+^J$ undesirable or bad outputs.

The DEA output set associated with the above data is

$$P(x) = \{ (y,b) : \sum_{k=1}^{K} z_k y_k \geq y, \text{ (single output)},$$

$$\sum_{k=1}^{K} z_k b_{kj} \leq b_j, j = 1, \ldots, J,$$

$$\sum_{k=1}^{K} z_k x_{kn} \leq x_n, n = 1, \ldots, N,$$

$$z_k \geq 0, k = 1, \ldots, K \}.$$

Given that the data meet the Kemeny et al. (1956) conditions discussed in Chapter 2,

$$\sum_{k=1}^{K} y_k > 0,$$

$$\sum_{k=1}^{K} x_{kn} > 0, n = 1, \ldots, N,$$

$$\sum_{n=1}^{N} x_{kn} > 0, k = 1, \ldots, K,$$

the technology $P(x)$ meets the axioms in Section 6.1. Since the intensity variables $z_k$, $k = 1, \ldots, K$ are only required to be nonnegative, the technology exhibits CRS (constant returns to scale), i.e.,

$$P(\lambda x) = \lambda P(x), \ \lambda > 0,$$

a condition we imposed to formulate our theorem in Section 6.1.

For the outputs $(y,b)$ to be null-joint, i.e.,

$$(y,b) \in P(x), b = 0 \Rightarrow y = 0,$$

we require that the bad outputs satisfy the following conditions

$$\sum_{k=1}^{K} b_{kj} > 0, \, j = 1,...,J,$$

$$\sum_{j=1}^{J} b_{kj} > 0, \, k = 1,...,K.$$

These state that each bad output is produced and each $k$ produces some bad output.

In this chapter, we will assume (the data is consistent with this) that each bad output is by itself null-joint with the single good output, i.e.,

$$(y, b_1 ... b_J) \in P(x), b_j = 0 \Rightarrow y = 0.$$

This condition holds when each $k$ produces all bad outputs

$$b_{kj} > 0 \text{ for each } k \text{ and } j, k = 1...K, j = 1,...,J.$$

To evaluate which bad is worst, we solve two linear programming problems for each $k$. The baseline output for $k'$ is

$$
\begin{aligned}
y_{k'}^{*} \;=\; & \max_{z_k, y} \; y \\[1mm]
s.t. \; & \sum_{k=1}^{K} z_k y_k \geq y, \\
& \sum_{k=1}^{K} z_k b_{kj} \leq b_{k'j}, \, j = 1,...,J, \\
& \sum_{k=1}^{K} z_k x_{kn} \leq x_n, \, n = 1,...,N \; \text{(free)}, \\
& x_n \geq 0, \, n = 1,...,N, \\
& z_k \geq 0, \, k = 1,...,K.
\end{aligned}
\tag{6.1}
$$

Note that each bad $b_{k'j}, \, j = 1...J$ is taken given as that the observed data and all inputs $x_n, \, n = 1...N$ are free to take any nonnegative value, which is what our theorem requires.

Our second problem estimates the maximal good output for observation $k'$, when in addition to inputs $b_1$ is free, i.e.,

$$\hat{y}_{k'}(b_1) = \max_{z_k, y} y$$

$$s.t. \quad \sum_{k=1}^{K} z_k y_k \geqq y,$$

$$\sum_{k=1}^{K} z_k b_{k1} \leqq b_1 \quad \text{(free)},$$

$$\sum_{k=1}^{K} z_k b_{kj} \leqq b_{k'j}, \, j = 2,...,J, \quad (6.2)$$

$$\sum_{k=1}^{K} z_k x_{kn} \leqq x_n, \, n = 1,...,N \quad \text{(free)},$$

$$z_k \geqq 0, \, k = 1,...,K,$$

$$x_n \geqq 0, \, n = 1,...,N.$$

A comparison of (6.1) and (6.2) yields the degree to which $b_1$ restricts good output for each observation in our sample.

To determine which bad is the worst in terms of loss of production, we can compare $\hat{y}_{k'}(b_1)$ (where bad $b_1$ is unregulated) and $y_{k'}^*$ (where all bads are regulated). For example, $\forall k'$:

$$Y_{k'}(b_1) = \frac{\hat{y}_{k'}(b_1) - y_{k'}^*}{y_{k'}^*} \cdot 100 \quad (6.3)$$

tells us by what percent firm $k'$ can increase good output production if the bad output $b_1$ is free from regulation.

Besides yielding the maximum good output when $b_1$ is not regulated, i.e., $\hat{y}_{k'}(b_1)$, the solution to (6.2) also yields the corresponding optimal bad output value, $\hat{b}_1$. By comparing $\hat{b}_{k'1}$ with the optimal baseline value $b_{k'1}^*$, we can calculate how much more a bad output could be produced if that bad is free from regulation. For example, $\forall k'$:

$$B_{k'}(b_1) = \frac{\hat{b}_{k'1} - b_{k'1}^*}{b_{k'1}^*} \cdot 100 \quad (6.4)$$

tells us the percent by which firm $k'$ could increase $b_1$ if it is free from regulation.

## 6.3   Data

Our model is applied to estimate the restrictiveness of regulations on bad outputs in Swedish industry using firm-level data especially compiled for our research by Statistics Sweden. We focus particularly on the pulp and paper industry, covering the period 1998 to 2008. The pulp and paper industry is subject to regulation of all three of the pollutants we are focusing on in the analysis: carbon dioxide ($CO_2$), sulfur dioxide ($SO_2$), and nitrogen oxides ($NO_x$).

The firms produce one good output, and this variable is created by dividing firm-level sales by a sector-level producer price index, which serves as a proxy for physical output (an output index). Bad outputs, $CO_2$, $SO_2$, and $NO_x$, are produced as by-products (measured in tons). As defined in Equations (6.1) and (6.2), our model considers inputs in production as being free, as long as they are non-negative. Inputs are real capital (machines and buildings), measured in million SEK,[6] number of employees, fossil fuels (coal, oil, gasoline), electricity,[7] and biofuels (including heat), where energy inputs are measured in MWh. The data for all variables used in the empirical application are summarized in Table 6.1.

*Table 6.1* Descriptive statistics, Swedish pulp and paper industry in 1998 and 2008

| Variables | Units | Mean | SD | Minimum | Maximum |
|---|---|---|---|---|---|
| 1998 (number of firms = 32) | | | | | |
| Good output | MSEK | 1852 | 2690 | 142 | 14620 |
| $CO_2$ | ton | 56427 | 56424 | 3742 | 253293 |
| $SO_2$ | ton | 104 | 112 | 5 | 495 |
| $NO_x$ | ton | 120 | 124 | 4 | 489 |
| Capital | MSEK | 1452 | 1825 | 48 | 7658 |
| Labor | Workers | 839 | 1183 | 94 | 6490 |
| Fossil fuels | MWh | 207002 | 207394 | 13652 | 923591 |
| Electricity | MWh | 488645 | 567306 | 10753 | 2384915 |
| Biofuel | MWh | 222798 | 264584 | 0 | 908665 |
| 2008 (number of firms = 33) | | | | | |
| Good output | MSEK | 2109 | 2201 | 257 | 10871 |
| $CO_2$ | ton | 36638 | 38585 | 1084 | 168368 |
| $SO_2$ | ton | 59 | 63 | 1 | 276 |
| $NO_x$ | ton | 110 | 115 | 1 | 460 |
| Capital | MSEK | 1787 | 1906 | 93 | 6812 |
| Labor | Workers | 611 | 628 | 83 | 3490 |
| Fossil fuels | MWh | 135365 | 141919 | 3951 | 616247 |
| Electricity | MWh | 652146 | 904564 | 67420 | 4350243 |
| Biofuel | MWh | 277126 | 305934 | 0 | 1135521 |

The average production of good output among the firms in the data set is nearly 14 percent higher in 2008 than in 1998. Capital use in production is approximately 23 percent higher and labor about 27 percent lower, which indicates a considerable increase in capital intensity. The electricity and biofuel use is about 33 percent and 24 percent higher, respectively, while the fossil fuel use is about 35 percent lower. Emissions of $CO_2$, $SO_2$, and $NO_x$ are about 35 percent, 43 percent, and 8 percent lower, respectively. By means of an emissions index,[8] Figure 6.2 illustrates the changes in the three emissions during the sample period for Swedish pulp and paper firms.

Overall, the emissions were decreasing from 2004 to 2008. $CO_2$ and $SO_2$ emissions have considerably decreased over this period. The $NO_x$ emissions were only slightly lower in 2008 compared to 2004.

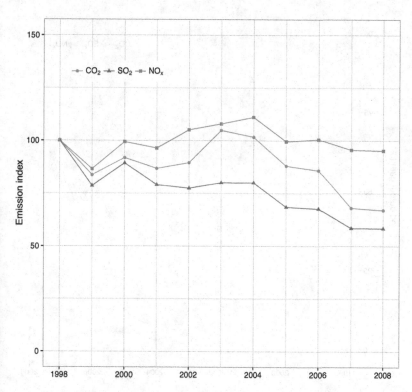

*Figure 6.2* Change in emissions of $CO_2$, $SO_2$, and $NO_x$ in Swedish pulp and paper industry between 1998 and 2008. (Index, 1998 = 100)

## 6.4   Results

Empirically, we study to what extent Swedish pulp and paper firms are restricted by bad outputs subject to regulation. Based on Equation (6.3), Figure 6.3 shows the potential output gains in the period 1998 to 2008, explicitly

$$\left\{ \sum_{k=1}^{K} \hat{y}_{k'}(b_1) - \sum_{k=1}^{K} y_{k'}^{*t} \middle/ \sum_{k=1}^{K} y_{k'}^{*t} \right\} \cdot 100, t = 1998, \ldots, 2008,$$

where $b_1$ indicates which of the three bads, $CO_2$, $SO_2$, or $NO_x$, is assumed free from regulation.

The potential output gain if $CO_2$ emissions were deregulated is clearly larger than that of either $SO_2$ or $NO_x$ during the period of study. This implies that the $CO_2$ regulation restricts the production of good output the most for the pulp and paper firms. Some gain in good output can also be attained if either $SO_2$ or $NO_x$ were deregulated. Since 2003, the potential output

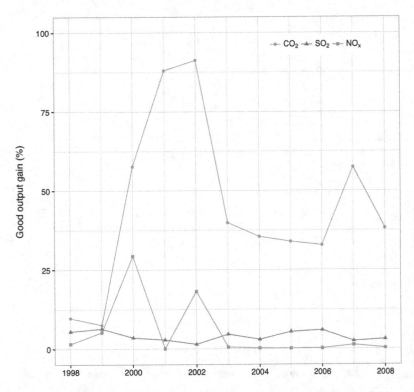

*Figure 6.3* Potential good output gain in percentage if one bad output, $CO_2$, $SO_2$, or $NO_x$, was deregulated, 1998–2008

gain by deregulating $SO_2$ has been only slightly larger than by deregulating $NO_x$. Additionally, the potential output gain from deregulating $NO_x$ has been close to zero.

Based on Equation (6.4), Figure 6.4 illustrates by what percent the firms could have increased each bad output if they were deregulated.

Figure 6.4 shows that the potential percentage increase in $CO_2$ emissions would exceed those of $SO_2$ and $NO_x$ under deregulation. It also shows that the potential increase in $NO_x$ emissions would be close to zero if it were deregulated. From a policy point of view, this implies that it would be possible to deregulate $NO_x$ without large increases in the quantity of $NO_x$ emissions.

To provide more detailed firm-level information from our results, we focus on the year 2008. The Salter Diagrams in Figure 6.5 show that individual firms experience the restrictiveness of bad outputs to a considerably varying degree. The counterfactual potential good output gain that could

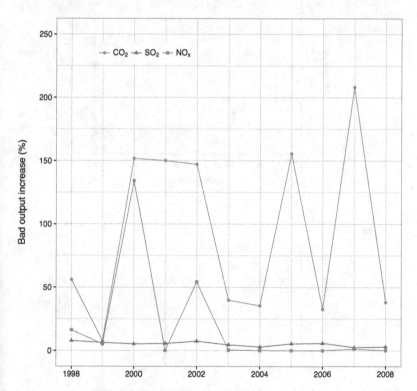

*Figure 6.4* Potential percentage increase in one bad output, $CO_2$, $SO_2$, or $NO_x$, if it was deregulated, 1998–2008

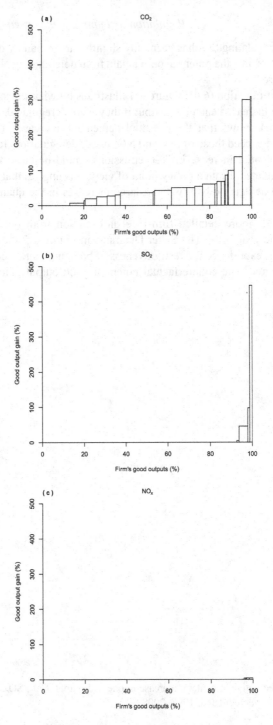

*Figure 6.5* Impact of regulations on $CO_2$, $SO_2$, $NO_x$ – the firm level, 2008

have been achieved in 2008 if the bad outputs were free from regulation are measured on the vertical axes. On the horizontal axes, the width of the columns illustrates the size of the individual firms as measured by the proportion of the firm's good output relative to total sector good output.

Figure 6.5a shows the outcome of $CO_2$ being deregulated. Almost all firms were adversely affected, as most of the firms could have increased production of good output if $CO_2$ were free from regulation. These firms produced nearly 70 percent of the good output totally produced, which indicates that firms that were restricted are larger on average than those that were not. Figures 6.5b and 6.5c show that only a few firms' good output is restricted by regulations on $SO_2$ and $NO_x$.

## 6.5 Conclusions

Industrial production causes emissions of undesirables that generate negative externalities. From the societal point of view, it is therefore of interest to implement environmental policy measures and regulate firms' emissions, or bad outputs. However, regulating bad outputs in industrial production may restrict firms in terms of foregone production of desirable outputs, or good outputs. In this chapter, we develop a DEA model to identify which bad is worst, i.e., the bad output that due to regulation most restricts firms' production of good outputs. The model can be used as an instrument to assess environmental regulations, e.g., by ranking the restriction of different types of bad output subject to different tax rates. We apply the model to Swedish pulp and paper data at the firm level, covering the period 1998 to 2008.

The results generally show that $CO_2$ was the most restrictive bad output measured by foregone production of good output due to regulation of $CO_2$ by tax or EU ETS during the period of study. Our results also show that $NO_x$ has only caused minor restrictions on production of good output. From a policy point of view, this indicates there was a potential for relaxing the regulation on $NO_x$. According to our results, this would result in only a small increase in total $NO_x$ emissions. Since $CO_2$, $SO_2$, and $NO_x$ emissions seem highly correlated, policies aimed at reducing $CO_2$ emissions would also contribute to reductions of $SO_2$ and $NO_x$. Thus, relaxing regulation on $NO_x$ may not induce large increases in $NO_x$ emissions. On the other hand, it may reduce administrative burden and save fees.

We provide an estimate of the individual impact on production of emission regulations in terms of foregone production of good outputs and potential increases in emissions under deregulation. Our approach focuses only on the effects of regulation of emissions on the firm. Optimal policy requires associated estimates on the external costs with respect to health impacts or environmental damages, for example.

## 6.6 Notes

1  In our empirical application, regulation is in the form of a tax on emissions – price rather than quantity regulation. See Weitzman (1974) for conditions under which these may have equivalent results.
2  For a survey of this law, see Färe (1980).
3  The discussion of technology with good and bad outputs closely follows Färe et al. (2013).
4  This notion is closely related to the concept of limitational inputs; see Shephard (1970a, b).
5  This condition may be weakened by, instead of requiring CRS, introducing output homotheticity.
6  The capital stock is created from firm-level data on gross investment by using the perpetual inventory method.
7  In Sweden, electricity is produced mainly by using non-fossil-intensive technologies, mainly hydro and nuclear power.
8  The emissions index is calculated according to, e.g., in the $CO_2$ case,

$$\sum\nolimits_{k=1}^{K} CO_2^{k,t} \bigg/ \sum\nolimits_{k=1}^{K} CO_2^{k,1998}, \ t = 1998,\ldots,2008.$$

## 6.7 References

Baumgärtner, S., H. Dykhoff, M. Faber, J. Proops, J. Shiller, 2001. The Concept of Joint Production and Ecological Economics. *Ecological Economics* 36: 365–372.
Färe, R., 1980. *Laws of Diminishing Returns, Lecture Notes in Economics and Mathematical Systems.* Vol. 176, Springer-Verlag, Berlin, 97 pages.
Färe, R., S. Grosskopf, 2004. *New Directions: Efficiency and Productivity.* Kluwer Academic Publishers, Boston.
Färe, R., S. Grosskopf, C. Pasurka, 2013. Joint Production of Good and Bad Outputs with a Network Application. *Encyclopedia of Energy, Natural Resources and Environmental Economics* 2: 109–118.
Johansen, L., 1968. Production Functions and the Concept of Capacity. Recherches Recentes sur le Fonction de Production, Collection, Mathematique et Econometrie 2.
Kemeny, J.G., O. Morgenstern, G.L. Thompson, 1956. A Generalization of the von Neumann Model of an Expanding Economy. *Econometrica* 24: 115–135.
Shephard, R.W., 1970a. Proof of the Law of Diminishing Returns. *Zeitschrift für Nationalökonomie* 30: 7–34.
Shephard, R.W., 1970b. *Theory of Cost and Production Functions.* Princeton University Press, Princeton.
Shephard, R.W., 1974. *Indirect Production Functions: Mathematical Systems in Economics, No. 10.* Verlag Anton Hain, Meisenheim Am Glan.
Shephard, R.W., R. Färe, 1974. The Law of Diminishing Returns. *Zeitschrift für Nationalökonomie* 34: 69–90.
Weitzman, M.L., 1974. Prices vs Quantities. *Review of Economic Studies* 41(4): 477–491.

# 7 Cost-benefit analysis with DEA

## Measuring expense effectiveness

### 7.1 Introduction

In previous chapters, we presented methods to assess the impact of environmental policy measures, which generally was about achieving better understanding of the impact on firms' productivity performance. We found that carbon taxation has influenced the Swedish manufacturing industry to produce more output per unit carbon emissions. We also found that economic policy instruments might have potential to spur firms to develop technologies. In this case, the change in environmental and economic performance, respectively, is driven by an exogenous factor beyond the firms' control, i.e., governmental intervention.

Governmental intervention may, e.g., take the form of taxes on emissions. By implementing taxes, the government burdens the firms with expenditures that give incentive to reduce emissions. In this chapter, we focus on the firms' perspective and propose a tool to analyze their environmental investment/expenditure budget and the potential to reduce emissions and, therefore, tax expenditures.

The tool is a cost-benefit analysis (CBA) framework, built on the cost indirect benefit function. We develop the tool generally, and then we formulate it as a data envelopment analysis (DEA) model, which allows us to compute outcomes using mathematical linear programming. In particular, we develop it as a short-run model by holding some inputs fixed. Emissions from production are treated as bad outputs whose quantities are chosen by the firms in order to optimize their economic performance given a fixed budget, which involves considering tax expenditures.

Examples of questions we are able to answer with this approach include:

- Given an increase in the price of fossil fuels due to a carbon tax introduction/increase, what is the optimal adaption in terms of increasing environmental or "green" investments?
- If government policy dictates that energy efficiency or productivity has to be improved by a certain percent, what is the optimal response, given this restriction, in terms of energy use and/or energy saving investment?

- What are the impacts of increasing environmental investments and expenditures on tax savings? This is the question we will look specifically at in our empirical illustration.

The tool reveals four different types of firms: (i) firms that can make no tax savings at all, not even through additional environmental protection expenditures; (ii) firms that can make tax savings without any additional expenditures; (iii) firms that can make unprofitable tax savings through additional expenditures; and finally (iv) firms that can make profitable tax savings through additional environmental expenditures. Some firms (i and iii) may find it unprofitable and hence not good for business. Accordingly, taxing emissions will not necessarily lead all firms to reduce emissions.

To illustrate the practical use of the analytical tool, we apply it to the Swedish pulp and paper industry in 2007 as an example.

## 7.2   Cost-benefit analysis and DEA

In this section, we introduce a short-run cost indirect output correspondence, which is our basic building block for our cost-benefit analysis model. We provide some basic properties of this model prior to constructing a DEA version. The latter is used for our estimations.

Let $x = (x_v, x_f) \in R_+^N$ be a vector of inputs, where $x_v$ denotes the subvector of variable inputs and $x_f$, fixed inputs. Outputs are denoted as a vector $y \in R_+^M$, and the output correspondence is modeled as

$$P(x_v, x_f) = \{y : (x_v, x_f) \text{ can produce } y\}.$$

In general, $P(x_v, x_f)$ is assumed to be a compact set with inputs and outputs strongly disposable; see Färe and Primont (1995) for details.

Let $C$ be the budget or allowed cost for variable inputs and let $w_v$ be their prices. The cost indirect output correspondence is defined as

$$IP(x_f, w_v / C) = \{y : y \in P(x_v, x_f), w_v x_v \leqq C\}$$

$$= \{y : y \in P(x_v, x_f), \frac{w_v}{C} x_v \leqq 1\},$$

and it is the envelope of the output sets for $x_f$ and the variable inputs $x_v$, not costing more than $C$. For its properties, see Shephard (1974) or Färe and Grosskopf (1994). In addition, we note that if

$$y = \min\{x_v, x_f\}$$

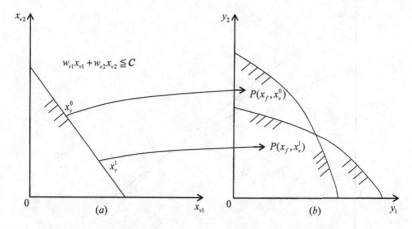

*Figure 7.1* The cost indirect output correspondence

Panel (a) illustrates the budget constraint, and each input vector (here two) maps into output space. The envelope of these output sets forms the cost indirect output correspondence.

where $x_v$ is the single variable input and $x_f$ is the single fixed input, $C^1 > C^0$ need not increase output. The reason is that $x_f$, as here, can be a limitational input.[1]

We illustrate the cost indirect output correspondence in Figure 7.1.

To model the benefit side of our cost benefit problem, let $p \in R_+^M$ be a vector of output prices, then consider the maximization problem

$$B(x_f, \frac{w_v}{C}, p) = \max\{ py : y \in IP(x_f, \frac{w_v}{C}) \}$$
$$= \max\{ py : y \in P(x_v, x_f), w_v x_v \leq C \}.$$

This cost indirect benefit function, $B(x_f, \frac{w_v}{C}, p)$, is illustrated in Figure 7.2.

The output vector that maximizes revenue is chosen from the feasible output vectors belonging to $IP(x_f, \frac{w_v}{C})$, in Figure 7.2 it is $y^*$.

We may now construct a cost benefit model as the ratio of benefit $B(x_f, \frac{w_v}{C}, p)$ to cost $C$, i.e.,

$$B(x_f, \frac{w_v}{C}, p) / C,$$

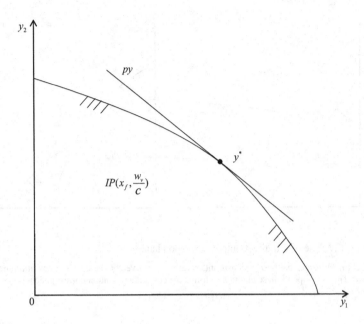

*Figure 7.2* The cost indirect benefit function

Equivalently, one may just use the benefit function,

$$B(x_f, \frac{w_v}{C}, p),$$

as a measure since it depends on $C$.

Turning next to the DEA/activity analysis version of our model, assume we have $k = 1,\ldots,K$ observations of inputs and outputs, $(x_v^k, x_f^k, y^k)$.

We construct our output correspondence $P(x_v, x_f)$ from the data as

$$P(x_v, x_f) = \{y: \sum_{k=1}^{K} z^k x_{vi}^k \leqq x_{vi}, i = 1,\ldots,I,$$

$$\sum_{k=1}^{K} z^k x_{fj}^k \leqq x_{fj}, j = 1,\ldots,J,$$

$$\sum_{k=1}^{K} z^k y_m^k \geqq y_m, m = 1,\ldots,M,$$

$$z^k \geqq 0, k = 1,\ldots,K\},$$

(7.1)

which has inputs and outputs strongly disposable and meets constant returns to scale. Constant returns to scale follows from the nonnegativity constraint on the intensity variables $z^k, k = 1,\ldots,K$. Input and output disposabilities are resulting from the three sets of inequalities.

Let $p \in R_+^M$ be an output price vector, $w_v$ prices on variable inputs and $C$ the allowed cost. We may then compute benefit/revenue for observation $k'$ as

$$\max_{y_m, x_{vi}, z^k} \sum_{m=1}^{M} p_m y_m$$

$$s.t. \quad \sum_{k=1}^{K} z^k x_{vi}^k \leqq x_{vi}, i = 1,\ldots,I,$$

$$\sum_{i=1}^{I} w_{vi} x_{vi} \leqq C^{k'}, \qquad (7.2)$$

$$\sum_{k=1}^{K} z^k x_{fj}^k \leqq x_{fj}^{k'}, j = 1,\ldots,J,$$

$$\sum_{k=1}^{K} z^k y_m^k \geqq y_m, m = 1,\ldots,M,$$

$$z^k \geqq 0, k = 1,\ldots,K,$$

where the second constraint is the allowable budget or cost constraint for observation $k'$. Note that in the maximization problem the fixed inputs and the allowed costs are specific for observation $k'$.

## 7.3 Measuring expense effectiveness

In this section, we modify our DEA cost-benefit model (7.2) so it can be applied to measure the benefit, for the tax savings from reducing $CO_2$ and $SO_2$ pollution, from a change in the environmental protection investment and current expenditure.

The data consists of five fixed inputs, capital $(K)$, labor $(L)$, fossil fuels $(F)$, renewable fuels $(R)$, and electricity $(E)$. Two undesirable outputs $CO_2$ $(C)$ and $SO_2$ $(S)$ are modeled as variable inputs (they are of course outputs), i.e., their inequalities are like those of inputs. In addition, we have one desirable output $Y$ and two types of expenditures (inputs): investment $(I)$ and current expenditure $(P)$, where these sum up to yield environmental protection expenditure $(B)$.

We also introduce the budget or environmental expenditure change $\Delta_B$, which can be allocated into investment change $\Delta_I$ and current expenditure change $\Delta_P$ so that $\Delta_I + \Delta_P \leq \Delta_B$. We use an inequality "$\leq$" to allow for "not spending it all". The consequences of the budget change are the changes in $CO_2$ pollution, $\Delta_C$, and $SO_2$ pollution, $\Delta_S$.

Let $t_C$ be the tax rate on $CO_2$ and $t_S$ the tax rate on $SO_2$, then we can compute the benefit or tax savings for observation $k'$ as

$$B_{k'} = \max_{\Delta_C, \Delta_S, \Delta_I, \Delta_P, z^k} t_C \Delta_C + t_S \Delta_S$$

$$s.t. \quad \sum_{k=1}^{K} z^k Y^k \geq Y^{k'},$$

$$\sum_{k=1}^{K} z^k K^k \leqq x_f^{k'}, x_f = K, L, F, R, E,$$

$$\sum_{k=1}^{K} z^k C^k \leqq C^{k'} - \Delta_C,$$

$$\sum_{k=1}^{K} z^k S^k \leqq S^{k'} - \Delta_S, \qquad (7.3)$$

$$\sum_{k=1}^{K} z^k I^k \leqq I^{k'} + \Delta_I,$$

$$\sum_{k=1}^{K} z^k P^k \leqq P^{k'} + \Delta_P,$$

$$\Delta_I + \Delta_P \leqq \Delta_B,$$

$$z^k \geqq 0, \quad k = 1, ..., K.$$

This model estimates the maximal tax savings (benefits), $t_C \Delta_C^* + t_S \Delta_S^*$, that can be obtained from a budget or environmental protection expenditure change $\Delta_B$.

## 7.4   Data

We apply our DEA cost-benefit model to the Swedish pulp and paper industry data in 2007. The data on the variables is collected and offered by Statistics Sweden (SCB). Environmental protection expenditures are the expenses paid by industrial firms each year for environmental protection.

*Table 7.1* Descriptive statistics, the Swedish pulp and paper industry in 2007

| Variables | Units | Mean | SD | Min | Max |
|---|---|---|---|---|---|
| Good output ($Y$) | MSEK | 2215 | 2218 | 256 | 11174 |
| $CO_2$ ($C$) | ton | 36832 | 38454 | 568 | 149191 |
| $SO_2$ ($S$) | ton | 56 | 62 | 1 | 257 |
| Capital ($K$) | MSEK | 2025 | 1983 | 97 | 6789 |
| Labor ($L$) | Workers | 681 | 643 | 131 | 3595 |
| Fossil fuels ($F$) | MWh | 135788 | 140005 | 2084 | 546534 |
| Renewable fuels ($R$) | MWh | 261590 | 300923 | 0 | 1196643 |
| Electricity ($E$) | MWh | 691973 | 893263 | 66808 | 4315473 |
| Environmental protection investment ($I$) | kSEK | 10771 | 14567 | 0 | 51700 |
| Current expenditure ($P$) | kSEK | 25190 | 26759 | 600 | 122785 |

This includes investment and current expenditure. To create a collection of approximately homogeneous firms, we choose only firms within the EU ETS, a total of 32 firms. The descriptive statistics of all the variables are summarized in Table 7.1. The complete data is provided in Appendix 7.

The $CO_2$ tax for Swedish industrial firms included in the EU ETS was gradually phased out starting in 2008. We use the EU ETS carbon price instead of carbon tax in our estimations. The carbon price is 0.006 SEK/kg $CO_2$ in 2007. The Swedish tax on $SO_2$ is 15 SEK/kg $SO_2$ in 2007.

## 7.5 Results

To estimate tax savings induced by a change in environmental protection expenditure (EPE), we first solve our DEA model (7.3) by specifying $\Delta_B$ to be 5 percent of the firm's observed EPE. The results are presented in Table 7.2. Column 1 (Tax) is the observed tax of $CO_2$ and $SO_2$ paid by the firms. Column 2 ($\Delta_B$) is the allowed budget change, assuming 5 percent of the firms' observed EPE. Columns 3–7 present the optimal solutions to the DEA model. The data in Column 8 are the ratios of tax saving ($B^*$) to the optimal budget change $\Delta_B^*$ ($=\Delta_I^* + \Delta_P^*$). Since our model allows for not spending the increased budget at all (see Section 7.3), $\Delta_B^* = 0$ is feasible, which implies that any marginal increase in the environmental expense may not lead to positive tax savings, *ceteris paribus*. The reason for this is that, as pointed out in Section 7.2, the fixed input variables, in our case capital, labor, and energy, are limitational. Consequently, $\Delta_B^* = 0$ when the constraints for the fixed variables are binding, and ratio of $B^*$ to $\Delta_B^*$ is undefined.

Table 7.2 A cost-benefit analysis on environmental protection expenditure. The Swedish pulp and paper industry firms in 2007 (5% more of the firm's observed environmental protection expenditure is allowed)

| Firm | Tax | $+\Delta_B$ | $+\Delta_I^*$ | $+\Delta_P^*$ | $-\Delta_C^*$ | $+\Delta_S^*$ | $B^*$ | $\frac{B^*}{\Delta_B^*}$ | $B_0$ | $\frac{B^*-B_0}{\Delta_B^*}$ |
|------|-----|-------------|---------------|---------------|---------------|---------------|-------|--------------------------|-------|------------------------------|
| | (kSEK) | (kSEK) | (kSEK) | (kSEK) | (ton) | (ton) | (kSEK) | | (kSEK) | |
| 1 | 97 | 60 | 0 | 0 | 0 | 0 | 0 | - | 0 | - |
| 2 | 113 | 125 | 0 | 0 | 0 | 0 | 0 | - | 0 | - |
| 3 | 330 | 440 | 0 | 0 | 0 | 0 | 0 | - | 0 | - |
| 4 | 331 | 335 | 0 | 0 | 0 | 0 | 0 | - | 0 | - |
| 5 | 542 | 1405 | 0 | 0 | 0 | 0 | 0 | - | 0 | - |
| 6 | 1386 | 2355 | 0 | 0 | 0 | 0 | 0 | - | 0 | - |
| 7 | 2458 | 402 | 0 | 0 | 0 | 0 | 0 | - | 0 | - |
| 8 | 3482 | 2460 | 0 | 0 | 0 | 0 | 0 | - | 0 | - |
| 9 | 3569 | 3048 | 0 | 0 | 0 | 0 | 0 | - | 0 | - |
| 10 | 4862 | 871 | 0 | 0 | 0 | 0 | 0 | - | 0 | - |
| 11 | 10954 | 3593 | 0 | 0 | 0 | 0 | 0 | - | 0 | - |
| 12 | 759 | 2825 | 0 | 0 | 1896 | 10 | 440 | - | 440 | - |
| 13 | 1848 | 663 | 0 | 0 | 8463 | 11 | 1464 | - | 1464 | - |
| 14 | 2481 | 772 | 0 | 0 | 9833 | 7 | 1624 | - | 1624 | - |
| 15 | 3634 | 533 | 0 | 0 | 16587 | 21 | 2875 | - | 2875 | - |
| 16 | 5669 | 2152 | 0 | 0 | 25565 | 7 | 4035 | - | 4035 | - |
| 17 | 6046 | 1206 | 0 | 0 | 22308 | 62 | 4366 | - | 4366 | - |
| 18 | 9913 | 3340 | 0 | 0 | 51902 | 90 | 9348 | - | 9348 | - |
| 19 | 14331 | 4156 | 0 | 0 | 75424 | 86 | 12910 | - | 12910 | - |
| 20 | 7042 | 2712 | 0 | 1313 | 31599 | 61 | 5783 | 4.40 | 5734 | 0.04 |
| 21 | 2435 | 43 | 24 | 19 | 60 | 0 | 10 | 0.23 | 0 | 0.23 |
| 22 | 12285 | 660 | 270 | 390 | 1045 | 2 | 186 | 0.28 | 0 | 0.28 |
| 23 | 3750 | 371 | 371 | 0 | 18833 | 31 | 3369 | 9.08 | 3310 | 0.16 |
| 24 | 2673 | 460 | 460 | 0 | 507 | 5 | 150 | 0.33 | 0 | 0.33 |
| 25 | 20925 | 2366 | 728 | 1638 | 2125 | 3 | 376 | 0.16 | 0 | 0.16 |
| 26 | 4738 | 767 | 767 | 0 | 22742 | 32 | 3975 | 5.18 | 3664 | 0.41 |
| 27 | 8262 | 1661 | 1140 | 0 | 43627 | 74 | 7834 | 6.87 | 7358 | 0.42 |
| 28 | 3773 | 3395 | 3395 | 0 | 16312 | 40 | 3116 | 0.92 | 719 | 0.71 |
| 29 | 26829 | 7074 | 7074 | 0 | 15473 | 165 | 4853 | 0.69 | 0 | 0.69 |
| 30 | 23309 | 4354 | 0 | 4306 | 99393 | 142 | 17432 | 4.05 | 4821 | 2.93 |
| 31 | 8633 | 351 | 351 | 0 | 4553 | 7 | 809 | 2.30 | 0 | 2.30 |
| 32 | 11141 | 2572 | 2572 | 0 | 22992 | 33 | 4028 | 1.57 | 1330 | 1.05 |

Note: $\Delta_B^* = \Delta_I^* + \Delta_P^*$; "-" means that the ratio is undefined since $\Delta_B^* = 0$.

Since there may exist inefficiency with respect to the reduction of $CO_2$ and $SO_2$ emissions in the production process by a firm, and since by improving efficiency it is possible to further reduce the emissions of $CO_2$ and $SO_2$ without requiring any additional EPE, we also calculate the potential tax savings, say $B_0$, from reductions in $CO_2$ and $SO_2$ emissions when inefficiency is removed. We estimate the value of $B_0$ by solving the DEA model again by setting $\Delta_B = 0$. The value of $B_0$ associated with each of the firms is provided in Column 9. Column 10 provides the ratio of net tax savings from a 5 percent change in EPE.

Analyzing the numerical results in the table, we can find four types of firms, when testing the assumed budget change for the sample firms.

I:   firms 1–11. The optimal value of $B^*$ for all these firms is 0. This implies that any additional EPE cannot reduce $CO_2$ and $SO_2$ emissions, *ceteris paribus*. This is to say, it is not possible for these firms to save tax by a marginal increase of EPE, while the other factors are fixed.

II:  firms 12–19. Positive values of $B_0$ are obtained for these firms. However, the sum of $\Delta_I^*$ and $\Delta_P^*$ is 0. This implies that even without demanding additional EPE, these firms still can reduce $CO_2$ and $SO_2$ emissions. The reason for such a reduction is that there is inefficiency with respect to the reduction of $CO_2$ and $SO_2$ emissions in production, as we mentioned previously. By improving efficiency, it is possible for these firms to further reduce the emissions of $CO_2$ and $SO_2$ without requiring any additional EPE and other factors.

III: firms 20–29. $B^*$ is larger than $B_0$, indicating that tax savings from reducing $CO_2$ and $SO_2$ pollution can be achieved from additional budget. However, the ratio of $(B^* - B_0)$ to $\Delta_B^*$ is less than 1, indicating that the tax savings cannot cover all the cost. In other words, these firms will make an economic loss, if they only spend more on their EPE.

IV:  firms 30–32. The ratio of $(B^* - B_0)$ to $\Delta_B^*$ is larger than 1, indicating that tax savings exceed the cost of reducing emissions. These firms can economically benefit from a marginal EPE increase without requiring any additional amount of capital, labor, and energy.

## 7.6   Concluding remarks

If society values emission reductions, the government can intervene by restricting emissions from firms' production processes. For example, taxes on emissions may incentivize firms to reduce emissions. In this chapter, we have proposed a tool to analyze firms' potential to reduce emission tax expenditures. To illustrate the practical use of the analytical tool, we applied it to 32 firms in the Swedish pulp and paper industry operating in 2007.

By assuming that firms would have been able to increase environmental protection expenditures by 5 percent, we computed how much firms could reduce emissions and achieve tax savings. The outcome shows that only about 10 percent of the firms would have benefitted from increasing environmental expenditures in order to reduce emissions and tax expenditures (firm type iv). However, some 25 percent of the firms actually had the opportunity to reduce emissions and tax expenditures without additional environmental expenditures (firm type ii). This reveals inefficiencies in production in terms of inefficiencies in management and/or firms not using the best practice technology. For 65 percent of the firms, there were no economic reasons to reduce emissions, as benefits from the tax savings would not have exceeded the 5 percent increase in expenditures (firm types i and iii). Thus, a general policy implication from the example given in this chapter is that implementing new, or increasing already existing, emission taxes does not necessarily trigger emission reductions, with or without additional environmental protection expenditures.

The analytical tool may also serve as a support for managers when operating more than one producing plant. In order to optimize the economic performance of a firm, the management can use the tool in order to identify which plant or plants could benefit from emission reductions and tax savings, with or without additional environmental production expenditures.

## 7.7 Note

1 In general for $y = F(x_1, x_2)$, $x_2$ is limitational if $\sup_{x_1 \geq 0} F(x_1, x_2) < +\infty$, for each $x_2 \geq 0$.

## 7.8 References

Färe, R., S. Grosskopf, 1994. *Cost and Revenue Constrained Production*. Bilkent University Lecture Series, Springer-Verlag, Berlin, 170 pages.
Färe, R., D. Primont, 1995. *Multi-Output Production and Duality: Theory and Applications*. Kluwer Academic Publishers, Boston.
Shephard, R.W., 1974. *Indirect Production Functions: Mathematical Systems in Economics, No. 10*. Verlag Anton Hain, Meisenheim Am Glan.

## 7.9 Appendix 7

Table A Swedish pulp and paper industry production data in 2007

| Firm | Output (Y) | $CO_2$ (C) (ton) | $SO_2$ (S) (ton) | Capital (K) (MSEK) | Labor (L) | Fossil fuel (F) (MWh) | Biofuel (R) (MWh) | Electricity (E) (MWh) | Investment (I) (kSEK) | Current expenditure (P) kSEK |
|---|---|---|---|---|---|---|---|---|---|---|
| 1 | 500 | 568 | 1 | 557 | 266 | 2084 | 0 | 75760 | 600 | 600 |
| 2 | 256 | 659 | 1 | 120 | 131 | 2402 | 0 | 148598 | 1500 | 1000 |
| 3 | 1402 | 1620 | 5 | 1388 | 456 | 5915 | 48932 | 353320 | 3950 | 4850 |
| 4 | 282 | 1736 | 4 | 97 | 140 | 6532 | 51575 | 93877 | 4069 | 2638 |
| 5 | 1146 | 3006 | 5 | 1248 | 311 | 10959 | 24207 | 326486 | 14514 | 13594 |
| 6 | 2206 | 6470 | 26 | 1825 | 746 | 23585 | 254175 | 532774 | 7463 | 39650 |
| 7 | 943 | 15894 | 1 | 139 | 300 | 67452 | 0 | 128274 | 2725 | 5321 |
| 8 | 2859 | 18437 | 43 | 2428 | 587 | 67661 | 348356 | 617863 | 20000 | 29200 |
| 9 | 3647 | 21112 | 21 | 4140 | 1028 | 78835 | 0 | 959379 | 8112 | 52853 |
| 10 | 1445 | 30284 | 13 | 798 | 587 | 123994 | 127881 | 152699 | 0 | 17421 |
| 11 | 3042 | 61996 | 94 | 2821 | 525 | 226139 | 302026 | 628139 | 1900 | 69972 |
| 12 | 321 | 3783 | 12 | 215 | 258 | 13803 | 102675 | 66808 | 51700 | 4800 |
| 13 | 376 | 10522 | 15 | 161 | 210 | 38472 | 51088 | 128855 | 6755 | 6511 |
| 14 | 614 | 15281 | 9 | 338 | 386 | 60856 | 5315 | 125786 | 3300 | 12156 |
| 15 | 688 | 21356 | 23 | 383 | 299 | 78997 | 0 | 232160 | 4251 | 6418 |
| 16 | 2899 | 34053 | 28 | 2714 | 836 | 151677 | 266635 | 1396985 | 14525 | 28521 |
| 17 | 1970 | 32058 | 74 | 1665 | 637 | 117785 | 531480 | 412679 | 7566 | 16556 |
| 18 | 2584 | 54868 | 98 | 3481 | 1061 | 200044 | 458081 | 730120 | 29800 | 37000 |
| 19 | 3485 | 83150 | 102 | 6111 | 998 | 253859 | 159520 | 2405859 | 41168 | 41954 |
| 20 | 1341 | 38295 | 76 | 1567 | 312 | 139600 | 431622 | 318993 | 41926 | 12315 |

(Continued)

Table A (Continued)

| Firm | Output (Y) | $CO_2$ (C) (ton) | $SO_2$ (S) (ton) | Capital (K) (MSEK) | Labor (L) | Fossil fuel (F) (MWh) | Biofuel (R) (MWh) | Electricity (E) (MWh) | Investment (I) (kSEK) | Current expenditure (P) (kSEK) |
|---|---|---|---|---|---|---|---|---|---|---|
| 21 | 876 | 14334 | 15 | 450 | 393 | 53163 | 0 | 284004 | 0 | 870 |
| 22 | 4873 | 67835 | 123 | 5079 | 1401 | 256087 | 821849 | 2506330 | 6150 | 7050 |
| 23 | 423 | 21143 | 33 | 301 | 143 | 77095 | 112820 | 266359 | 1144 | 6278 |
| 24 | 1017 | 14026 | 34 | 477 | 336 | 51131 | 244558 | 252986 | 0 | 9210 |
| 25 | 5025 | 120931 | 153 | 4597 | 1115 | 458255 | 607490 | 943991 | 0 | 47328 |
| 26 | 498 | 27616 | 32 | 195 | 313 | 100814 | 0 | 240600 | 1067 | 14287 |
| 27 | 1792 | 45738 | 81 | 1760 | 643 | 172383 | 536756 | 491313 | 3996 | 29233 |
| 28 | 2304 | 19692 | 49 | 2339 | 830 | 72398 | 379005 | 529700 | 2858 | 65061 |
| 29 | 11174 | 149191 | 257 | 4963 | 3595 | 546534 | 1196643 | 4315473 | 18700 | 122785 |
| 30 | 5538 | 130512 | 214 | 6789 | 1325 | 475875 | 845177 | 1186861 | 41605 | 45482 |
| 31 | 1304 | 50277 | 59 | 678 | 480 | 183279 | 0 | 256793 | 0 | 7037 |
| 32 | 4035 | 62177 | 104 | 4960 | 1144 | 227547 | 463029 | 1033306 | 3315 | 48132 |
| AVG | 2215 | 36832 | 56 | 2025 | 681 | 135788 | 261590 | 691973 | 10771 | 25190 |

# Index

Printed in the United States
by Baker & Taylor Publisher Services